GW00702297

Development
and Rights

Selected essays from
Development in Practice

Introduced by **Firoze Manji**

A Development in Practice Reader

Series Editor: **Deborah Eade**

Oxfam GB

First published by Oxfam GB in 1998
Reprinted by Oxfam GB in 1999

© Oxfam GB 1998

ISBN 0 85598 406 6

A catalogue record for this publication is available from the British Library.

Available from the following agents:
USA: Stylus Publishing LLC, PO Box 605, Herndon, VA 20172-0605, USA
tel: +1 (0)703 661 1581; fax: + 1(0)703 661 1547; email: styluspub@aol.com
Canada: Fernwood Books Ltd, PO Box 9409, Stn. 'A', Halifax, N.S. B3K 5S3, Canada
tel: +1 (0)902 422 3302; fax: +1 (0)902 422 3179; e-mail: fernwood@istar.ca
India: Maya Publishers Pvt Ltd, 113-B, Shapur Jat, New Delhi-110049, India
tel: +91 (0)11 649 4850; fax: +91 (0)11 649 1039; email: surit@del2.vsnl.net.in
K Krishnamurthy, 23 Thanikachalan Road, Madras 600017, India
tel: +91 (0)44 434 4519; fax: +91 (0)44 434 2009; email: ksm@md2.vsnl.net.in
South Africa, Zimbabwe, Botswana, Lesotho, Namibia, Swaziland:
David Philip Publishers, PO Box 23408, Claremont 7735, South Africa
tel: +27 (0)21 64 4136; fax: +27(0)21 64 3358; email: dppsales@iafrica.com
Tanzania: Mkuki na Nyota Publishers, PO Box 4246, Dar es Salaam, Tanzania
tel/fax: +255 (0)51 180479, email: mkuki@ud.co.tz
Australia: Bush Books, PO Box 1958, Gosford, NSW 2250, Australia
tel: +61 (0)2 043 233 274; fax: +61 (0)2 092 122 468, email: bushbook@ozemail.com.au

Rest of the world: contact Oxfam Publishing, 274 Banbury Road, Oxford OX2 7DZ, UK.
tel. +44 (0)1865 311 311; fax +44 (0)1865 313 925; email publish@oxfam.org.uk

Typeset in Melior, printed by Litho & Digital Impressions Ltd (LDi).

Published by Oxfam GB, 274 Banbury Road, Oxford OX2 7DZ, UK

Oxfam GB is a registered charity, no. 202 918, and is a member of Oxfam International.

Dedicated to the memory of our dear colleague and *compañera*, Christine Whitehead, who died in July 1998. She fought tirelessly for the cause of social and economic justice in Latin America and elsewhere.

Contents

Preface

Deborah Eade

If the concept of universal, indivisible, and inalienable human rights — that body of rights and freedoms which belong to all people and peoples by virtue of their humanity — is not universally acknowledged, its corollary — that of the right to development — is more contested still. For almost the entire half-century since the signing of the Universal Declaration of Human Rights (UDHR), international political debate both on human rights and on development has been mediated by the ideological battle between the Cold War super-powers. Until 1989 and beyond, such debates were characterised on both sides by appeals to crude, monolithic stereotypes and self-serving rhetoric, further fuelled by mutual fears and hostilities, in which the contesting parties assumed the moral high ground rather than seeking to listen to or learn from each other. The nuclear arms race, and the policy of mutually assured destruction (aptly known by its acronym, MAD) ensured that proxy wars between the two powers were fought in the South.

A bipolar worldview requires and fosters false dichotomies and intellectual dishonesty, such as that epitomised in the notorious distinction claimed by Jeanne Kirkpatrick, a leading light in the Reagan Administration, between 'authoritarian' military regimes friendly to the USA (such as those of Pinochet, Somoza, or Ríos Montt) and the supposedly 'totalitarian' dictatorships of those such as Fidel Castro, Maurice Bishop, or Daniel Ortega. Thus the West, it was claimed by its critics, stood for individual rather than collective rights, for the rights of private capital over those of the common good, propping up military dictatorships in order to protect its political and economic influence. The Soviet bloc and China, on the other hand, were held to have achieved social and economic gains by trampling on the political and civil rights of individuals and of groups, and exerting an iron grip on their citizens.

Today, the ideological battle-lines are drawn differently. With the collapse of the USSR and the absence of a credible socialist alternative, there is no focal point for resistance to the ascendancy of neo-liberalism. Deregulation and anti-Statism are the order of the day. Indeed, in the 1990s, many of the former Soviet-bloc countries have (more or less willingly) undergone the 'shock therapy' of transition to market economies and privatisation, while those in the South were by the mid-1980s already (more or less reluctantly) embarked on the same process via economic structural adjustment. For their part, the international development agencies (and, by extension, their local counterparts) have increasingly adopted the conditionalities of 'good governance' and 'democratisation' to foster a somewhat narrow interpretation of political and civil rights. Meanwhile, with new divisions of labour emerging between State and non-State actors, social and cultural rights (and 'participation') are to be taken care of by 'civil-society organisations', including non-government organisations (NGOs), while economic rights are meted out via the free market. So much for the indivisibility of human rights. In addition, given the fast-diminishing role of national governments in regulating global markets which include everything from public utilities to fast-food chains and genetic material, it is unclear how individuals, groups, communities, or even nation-States will be able to defend the basic rights and fundamental freedoms that are enshrined in the UDHR.

Critiques of the universality of human rights often centre around the fact that, although the UDHR was ratified by the UN General Assembly in 1948, the worldview it represents is historically grounded in the liberal philosophical and political traditions of western Europe. As such, it is argued, the specificities of other cultures and thought systems are not adequately accommodated. However, despite sharp differences among delegates from North and South, the 1993 World Conference on Human Rights re-affirmed the universal, indivisible, and inalienable nature of human rights, including that of the right to development. Further, in the wake of shocking revelations concerning the use of mass rape as a military tactic in contemporary civil warfare, women's groups succeeded in having 'crimes of gender' acknowledged as a war crime; and in getting international acceptance for the appointment of a UN Special Rapporteur on Violence Against Women. But at the Fourth International Women's Conference held in Beijing in 1995, many Southern women's groups retreated from re-affirming the universality of human rights (and from the Vienna slogan 'Women's Rights are Human Rights'), arguing instead that, from their perspective, a 'gender and development' analysis would call for a complete re-conceptualisation of the notion of rights. In other spheres too, special-interest lobbies have multiplied, some seeking to have their rights explicitly incorporated into existing formulations and legislative structures, others proposing the radical overhaul of the latter. Another version, one might say, of revisionism versus revolutionary change; but one that is marked by a wider retreat — at least in many industrialised economies—from collective struggle into 'personal politics'.[1]

Political battles are ultimately waged by people organising either to protect what they have, or to fight for what they (or those whom they represent) need or wish to have. Many such battles — whether for land, work, decent housing, or for political expression, freedom of movement and association — are reflected in the papers gathered in this volume. However, the 1990s have also seen a widespread fragmentation of popular struggles, towards a necessary recognition of diversity and difference and away from the 'false universalisms'[2] of an earlier age — but perhaps into cultural relativism, and the 'commoditisation' or privatisation of values and struggles of a post-modern era. Where, in practice, does this leave a concept such as that of the right to development? And how can such a right be realised?

On the one hand, as Firoze Manji argues in his introductory essay, the development discourse has served to deflect the more radical, rights-based forms of mobilisation that spear-headed the liberation struggles in many countries. Instead of exercising their right to participate in shaping their societies, people are at best offered the opportunity to participate in top-down development projects that all too often act as a vehicle by which their existing rights and values are still further undermined. However, there are dangers in simply abandoning the notion that '[a] development strategy that disregards or interferes with human rights is the very negation of development'.[3] While there are serious problems with the description of an entire nation as 'under-developed', the reality is that a vast and growing number of human beings worldwide lack even the basic necessities of life. For all their limitations, the inter-government and non-government development organisations and numerous rights-based agencies have helped to ensure that these people, and the processes of impoverishment, do not disappear off the map of international consciousness. It is certainly possible to argue, as leading Southern thinkers such as Arturo Escobar and Gustavo Esteva have done,[4] that 'development' should be laid to rest rather than endlessly resuscitated by new qualifying adjectives — 'sustainable', 'people-centred', 'bottom-up', or 'participatory'. In various ways, many have also maintained that 'development' requires, creates, and perpetuates 'under-development': if competition is the name of the game, there will always be more losers than winners, and 'mal-development' is the result. As Firoze Manji puts it, there is no 'neutral territory' in addressing the causes of poverty and oppression. But, while it is clear that there can be no one way — no context-free solution — to these realities, there is still a need for a principled and consensual basis upon which to interpret the world, work out where we stand within it, and decide how and on whose side we wish to act. The UDHR is of necessity an imperfect instrument, a starting-point rather than a final destination. The discourse on human rights has been, and will doubtless continue to be, manipulated in cynical ways by governments and politicians concerned to protect their own narrow interests. A case in point is the discrepancy between the US response to alleged abuses of human rights in Cuba, which is of little or no economic significance to it, and to similar allegations of abuse in China, which happens to represent a vast potential market. Nevertheless, the UDHR represents a set of values that has given women and men from cultures as diverse as those of Algeria, Indonesia, or Mexico the courage to stand up to injustice and abuse, just as it has inspired ordinary people around the world to mobilise in solidarity with their struggles. It has been said that if women's social, political, and economic status reflected their numbers and the importance of their labour, the values shaping our global institutions would be profoundly altered.[5] Similarly, if the one-fifth of humanity who are today disenfranchised by virtue of absolute poverty could achieve even the most modest realisation of the rights enumerated in the existing Declaration, their collective voice would provide the moral basis upon which to build a broader and deeper understanding of the nature of human rights.

Notes

1 While the 1970s feminist insight that 'the personal is political' sought to break down the patriarchal distinction between the public space and private experience, it is today common to hear the argument that only those who personally belong to a particular interest group can represent or identify with its concerns. In the UK at least, it is certainly possible that this trend is in some way a response to the dismantling of the welfare state. However, the focus on ever-narrower identities can lead to an exclusive emphasis on what divides people rather than on what they have in common, and to a denial of the role of solidarity across social and other distinctions.

2 Anne Phillips (1991): *Engendering Democracy*, Cambridge: Polity Press, p. 168.

3 From the 1991 UN document 'The Realisation of the Right to Development', quoted in Deborah Eade and Suzanne Williams (1995): *The Oxfam Handbook of Development and Relief*, Oxford: Oxfam, p.24.

4 In *The Post-Development Reader*, edited by Majid Rahnema and Victoria Bawtree (London: Zed Books, 1997).

5 See, in particular, *UNDP: Human Development Report 1995*, New York: Oxford University Press.

The depoliticisation of poverty

Firoze Manji

1998 marks the fiftieth anniversary of the Universal Declaration of Human Rights (UDHR), which emerged from the triumph over genocide in Europe. Ironically the anniversary occurs in the aftermath of genocide in Africa which claimed the lives of more than one million men, women, and children in the space of nine months. It was a tragedy made more painful by the criminal failure of the international community to take action to prevent its occurrence or to deal effectively with its consequences.

Reflecting on the achievements of the last 50 years, some might be forgiven for feeling that the UDHR offers little cause for celebration. That is not to say that there have not been victories over that period. But in spite of them, the conditions of the people of the Third World are desperate. The social gains of independence from colonial rule have been rapidly eroded, as economies collapse under the combined weight of debt and structural adjustment programmes. Meanwhile the rich get richer, the poor poorer. While the average income of the top 20 per cent of the world's population was 30 times higher than that of the bottom 20 per cent in 1960, by 1994 it was 78 times higher. Nearly one quarter of the world's people have an income that is less than US$1 a day — a proportion which is rising. Each year, the UN Development Programme (UNDP) calculates the human-poverty index, based on a series of measures including the prevalence of illiteracy, life expectancy, degree of malnourishment, and access to health services and safe water. In 1996 over one billion people fell below this point, the position deteriorating in 30 countries; these were the worst figures since UNDP began calculating the index in 1990 (UNDP, 1997). Development, it seems, is failing.

The anniversary occurs in the context also of increasing number of conflicts in Africa. Such conflicts are frequently portrayed as being the result of apparently 'irreconcilable ethnic differences' which not only pervade the continent today, but are also viewed as intrinsic to its history. Mass violations of human rights are seen, therefore, as an 'inevitable', if regrettable, consequence of these 'ethnic' conflicts.

Growing impoverishment and conflict, and the increasing incidence of apparently ethnically based violence, have a common origin. They are the products of a process which began as popular mobilisation against oppression and exploitation—a movement for rights—which ultimately became warped into a process which became known as 'development'. Far from helping to overturn the social relations which reproduced injustice and impoverishment, the main focus of development was to discover and implement solutions which would enable the victims to cope with impoverishment, or find 'sustainable' solutions for living with it. Over the last few decades, development NGOs have played a critical role in that process. Their roles have gradually changed from articulating an embryonic anti-imperialism to becoming an integral part of post-colonial social formations.

Africa is a lens which discloses the general characteristics of development. The features are not particular to that continent. They are to be found also in Asia and Latin America, albeit tinted by the specific histories of those regions. By focusing on Africa, the complex inter-relationships between rights, poverty, and development can be revealed, with the knowledge that those in Asia and Latin America will hear resonances which chime with their own experience.

This paper discusses the historical processes which transformed the struggle for rights in Africa into an arena for a particular model of development. That model itself is, it is argued, the cause of some of the major conflicts which have arisen in Africa, including those which led to the genocide in Central Africa. The role of NGOs in the depoliticisation of poverty is examined in the context of these developments.

From rights to 'development'

The story of independence in Africa is frequently portrayed as the story of the machinations of nationalist leaders in mobilising popular agitations against the colonial powers, and their prowess at the negotiation tables. What is frequently omitted in such an account is the story of what was happening on the ground, in the forests, villages, urban ghettos, classrooms, and workplaces, in spite of—not because of—these leaders.

The period following the Second World War witnessed an unprecedented level of popular mobilisations and the formation of numerous popular organisations throughout the continent. Such developments were informed at the grassroots not so much (at least, not initially) by desires for abstract concepts of self-determination, but more by struggles for basic rights that wêre part of the everyday experiences of the majority. The initial spark for most people was provided by the desire to organise to claim rights to food, shelter, water, land, education, and health care, and the rights to freedom of association, freedom of speech, freedom of movement, freedom from harassment and other forms of human-rights abuses.[1] Different social groups focused on issues with which they were themselves most preoccupied — aspiring local capitalists organising to oppose restraints on their freedom to accumulate, while squatters organised to claim their rights of access to land.

It was these civil agitations (urban and rural) which provided the impetus to the liberation movements. Political independence was achieved through the ability of the leadership of the nationalist movements to capture the imagination of these formations, uniting them in the promise that only through self-determination and independence could all their aspirations be achieved.

The struggle for independence in Africa was thus informed, at the base, by the experience of struggles against oppression and brutal exploitation experienced in everyday life. These struggles constituted the emergence of a tradition of struggles for rights which was organic to and informed by the specific histories and experiences of those involved. Just as the bourgeois revolution which brought the capitalist class into ascendancy in Europe led to the emergence of a particular construct of rights proclaimed against the *ancien régime*, so Africa's struggle against the colonial yoke gave birth to its own traditions of struggle and the construct of rights. The concept of rights was not something that was 'God-given' in its universality, but forged in the fires of anti-imperialist struggles. It was informed by the need to overthrow all forms (not just colonial) of oppression and exploitation, not by constructs which had either been embodied in the UDHR or imported into Africa by those nationalist leaders who had spent periods in exile or study in the imperial homeland.

These struggles laid the basis in many countries for the emergence of a national consciousness which would provide some legitimacy to the nation-State that was about to be established. But that dynamic was not to be permitted to reach its logical conclusion. While the liberation struggles had begun the process of forging a common national identity, this identity remained fragile at the time of transfer of power, even in those countries (such as Mozambique, Angola, and Guinea Bissau) which had to undergo protracted wars of liberation.

Once thrown into power, the nationalist leadership (composed usually of representatives of the newly emerging middle class) saw its task as one of preventing 'centrifugal forces' from competing for political power or seeking greater autonomy from the newly formed 'nation'. Having grasped political self-determination from colonial authority, it was reluctant to accord the same rights to others. The new controllers of the State machinery saw their role as the 'sole developer' and 'sole unifier' of society. The State defined for itself an interventionist role in 'modernisation' and a centralising and controlling role in the political realm.

Born out of a struggle for the legitimacy of pluralism against a hegemonic colonial State, social pluralism began to be frowned upon. The popular associations which had projected the nationalist leadership into power gradually began to be seen as an obstacle to the new god of 'development'. No longer was there a need, it was argued, for popular participation in determining the future. The new government would bring development to the people. The new government, they claimed, represented the nation and everyone in it. Now that political independence had been achieved, the priority was 'development'. Social and economic improvements would come with patience and as a result of combined national effort involving all classes (*harambee*, in Kenyatta's famous slogan). In this early period after independence, civil and political rights soon came to be seen as a 'luxury', to be enjoyed at some unspecified time in the future when 'development' had been achieved. For the present, said many African presidents, 'our people are not ready' — echoing, ironically, the arguments used by the former colonial rulers against the nationalists' cries for independence a few years earlier.

In the colonial era, government social services for Africans were almost non-existent. Where they were provided, the purpose was largely to ensure the integrity of the structures of colonial rule. In periods of serious outbreaks of epidemics in the shanty-towns and over-crowded ghettos, health services were provided principally to stave off the possibilities of infections spreading into white society. In some instances, limited education was provided when certain basic skills would be necessary for the administration of the colony or for the particular forms of exploitation. For the vast majority of the rural population, it was left to a clutch of charities and missionary groups (what in today's jargon would be recognised as NGOs) to exchange their spiritual wares for material support in education, health, or other social services. For white settlers or the agents of colonial rule, however, State expenditure on the social sector was usually generous. Although on the eve of independence there were to be significant changes in the extent to which investments were to be made in the social sectors, for the most part the State's function in these sectors was to provide only for a minority.

The situation was to change dramatically at independence. It remains one of the most remarkable, and yet least acknowledged, achievements of independence governments that, within the space of but a few years, access to health services and to education was to become effectively universal. No matter how much one may criticise the forms of services provided,[2] it is a tribute to the capacity of the State to implement such far-reaching social programmes. While NGOs may today debate and shower praises on each other for their own capacities to 'scale-up', the new governments at independence implemented programmes of 'scaling-up' in a manner that no NGO has ever dared contemplate.[3] The impacts of these interventions are undeniable and were to be reflected in the subsequent dramatic changes in average life expectancy, in infant and child mortality rates, and in the improvements in nutritional status of the young. Huge improvements in all these parameters were to be observed throughout the continent by the end of the 1970s as a result of these social programmes. Aggregate figures for Sub-Saharan Africa show, for example, that life expectancy increased from 38 years in 1960 to 47 years in 1978, despite the fact that GNP per capita increased only modestly from US$222 to US$280 (World Bank, 1981).

But at the same time as this infrastructure was being built (often with the financial support of official aid agencies), a transformation had taken place which led to a demobilisation of the popular movement which had given rise to independence. Popular organisations which had emerged out of the struggle for rights (social, political, economic, or civil) were provided no further role in the process. Rights were no longer the flag around which the oppressed could rally. Indeed, the concept of rights was codified and rarefied in laws and constitutions whose relevance or application was determined by the self-proclaimed, and increasingly unaccountable, guardians of the State. A gradual shift took place, so that concerns about rights and justice were replaced by concerns about 'development'. Certainly there were major problems faced by the newly independent States in addressing how the forces of production (whether industrial or agricultural) could be developed to drag Africa out of the destitution created by colonial rule. But the discourse was not about development in the sense of developing the productive forces. It was about creating an infrastructure which advanced the capacity of the new ruling class to accumulate, and smoothing away those inefficiencies that hampered the capacity of international capital to continue its exploitation. It was expected that, through trickle-down effects, poverty would gradually be eliminated. This was the agenda of 'modernisation', the paradigm of development which was to hold sway until the end of the 1970s.

Central to this paradigm was to see 'poverty', rather than rights and freedom, as the main problem facing 'developing countries'. The victims of years of injustices, whose livelihoods had been destroyed by years of colonial rule, were now defined as 'the problem',[4] and thus the stage was set for the entry of the development NGO to participate in the process of depoliticising poverty. In Kenya, for example, peasants had been uprooted from their land and forced to eke out a living in marginal land with low yield-potential and which required immense labour to produce. The new paradigm required that ways be found to enable them to find sustainable (and participatory) approaches for surviving on such land. The need for carrying out land reform which would overcome the injustices created by colonialism was gradually forgotten.

The structures of accountability and democracy which were inherent in the movements centred on rights were gradually marginalised and replaced by the ascendancy of the expert, supported by bureaucratic and centralised decision-making under the guise of 'national planning'. Political associations were soon to be discouraged, if not actually banned, while trade unions were constrained, incorporated into the structures of the ruling party, or simply disbanded. In many countries, those structures which had emerged to organise around basic rights had all been either subsumed under 'development' or discarded within ten years of independence. The political hegemony of the new post-independence rulers had been asserted. Their capacity to attend to the 'basic needs' of the population gave them some legitimacy and allowed, in some instances, reasonable national cohesion. But the development of national consciousness, born fragile and imperfect in the struggle for rights in the 1950s and 1960s, began to lose sustenance, its life-blood dissipating. The age of the development expert, the relief expert, and subsequently the conflict-resolution expert, had arrived.

It is true that, in the early period, there had been a fairly broad moral and humane discourse. Nyerere, Senghor, Kaunda, Houphouet Boigny and others articulated their ideas on development or socialism usually in moral terms, with a discourse about African socialism being concerned with sharing, solidarity, and the common good. But, in practice, appeals to morality failed to address the structural issues related to the integration of the economies into the international economic order, which continued, albeit in a new form, to extract wealth from Africa into the hands of multinationals in the imperial heartland. It also failed to deal with the fact that those in control of the State and its organs had discovered that power and access provided by the State machinery was a significant source of wealth and private accumulation. While those like Nyerere sought to control the capacity of functionaries using the State as a source of accumulation, in many other countries such restraint was largely unknown. Access to the State as a source or means for accumulation of private wealth became an end in itself among the elite, the emerging ruling class. Favour, patronage, and frank corruption were seen as means for limiting competition to the honey-pot. And in many cases the most cohesive force able to compete for access to the State was the military. Certainly in West and Central Africa, *coups d'état* became (and sadly remain) commonplace.

But the 'misuse' of the State was to become a critical factor in the distortions brought to the development agenda. Patronage was used frequently to buy favours with different groups in the country. The purpose of development programmes was distorted to ensure that progress was brought not to where there was the greatest social or economic need, but instead to where investment would serve the need to curry favour with particular social or 'ethnic' groups whose political alliance was deemed useful at a particular time, and where the possibilities for private accumulation by the elite were greatest. Under such conditions, it was hardly surprising that competition for access to resources increasingly manifested itself along 'ethnic' lines. With the demise or suppression of organisations based on the struggle for rights, old social alliances based on perceived historical grievances against other 'ethnic' groups re-emerged. The seeds of subsequent conflicts were already taking root.

The emergence of the post-colonial State

The State in contemporary Africa inherited many of the features of its colonial predecessor. The repressive nature of colonial legislation, of the judiciary, and the coercive machinery of the State, is well documented. Colonial governance was authoritarian and racist. Its strategy of divide and rule was accompanied by uneven development.

After an initial zealousness which resulted in confrontations with pre-existing structures of African societies, colonial powers focused their attention on finding mechanisms for maintaining power through the manipulation and recasting of existing 'customary' structures or dominant tribes to defend or reinforce their own control. The complex inter-relations between and within different social formations which had emerged over thousands of years were cynically transformed, fossilised, or re-constituted into a caricature of their traditional structures. Those 'customary' leaders who were amenable to meeting the needs of the invading European State (be the need for slaves, for Africa's rich mineral wealth, for agricultural production, or as an outlet for over-production of commodities in Europe) were nurtured, and power was delegated to them for the vicarious maintenance of law and order. 'Decentralised despotism', to use Mamdani's brilliant characterisation (Mamdani, 1996), involved the extensive use of Native Authorities both to define and enforce custom, backed up by the armed might of the central State, as the means for controlling, governing, and exploiting rural peasantry. The colonial order made it necessary for the State to direct, even if through a combination of brute force and market forces, all spheres of life and to control the economy and the people in the interest of colonial exploitation. In the process, most fundamental human rights were frequently violated. Even after the adoption of UDHR in 1948, most of Africa was to be *de facto* excluded for at least a further decade from claiming the rights of humanity that were proclaimed in within it.[5]

Although those who commanded the State were replaced at independence, the structures of the State machinery were rarely transformed in any substantial or radical way. They were already intimately integrated into the capitalist world economy before independence, and there were to be no major shifts in the forms of production established within the country, nor changes to the terms of trade with the advanced capitalist countries (Barratt Brown, 1995). The economic framework of 'under-development' was left unchanged (Rodney, 1976). Despite much flag-waving and pontificating about socialism (and in some cases about 'Marxism-Leninism'), the social relations of production remained firmly within the framework of the capitalist world economy (Mandel, 1975).

The political programme that was carried out with considerable determination in virtually every country was to deracialise both the State and the public domain. Racially determined privilege was thoroughly overhauled, opening up for the ascendant middle classes new opportunities for private accumulation, creating the basis upon which favour and corruption would in due course flourish. But that process was primarily to change the face of urban life and urban civil society.

The structures of ethnically defined Native Authorities which constituted a critical tool of imperial domination before independence were, however, largely left intact in most countries. The deracialisation of urban life, without a concurrent detribalisation of rural authority, was to become the critical dichotomy of post-colonial political economy, and would be the source of major conflicts in future. For:

> ... Without a reform in the local state, the peasantry locked up under the hold of a multiplicity of ethnically defined Native Authorities could not be brought into the mainstream of the historical process. In the absence of democratisation, development became a top–down agenda enforced on the peasantry. Without thoroughgoing democratisation, there would be no development of the home market. The latter failure opened wide what was a crevice at independence. With every downturn in the international economy, the crevice turned into an opportunity for an externally defined structural adjustment that combined a narrowly defined program of privatisation with a broadly defined program of globalisation. The result was both an internal privatisation that recalled the racial imbalance that was civil society in the colonial period and an externally managed capital inflow that towed alongside a phalanx of expatriates—according to the UN estimates, more now than in the colonial period. (Mamdani, 1996: 288).

Structural adjustment and the rise of conflicts

The economic crisis which emerged out of the 'oil crisis' was characterised by a huge glut of capital. Europe and the USA were suddenly awash with capital, with few opportunities for high rates of return. Although many African countries already had heavy debts (Payer, 1989). there is little doubt that the surfeit of capital created by the oil crisis provided a qualitative encouragement to increase the debt burden. As a result, developing countries were courted to take loans to finance 'development'. Although the absolute size of debt of sub-Saharan African countries was relatively small in proportion to the external indebtedness of many developing countries, the size of the debt (and the cost of servicing that debt) in relation to the resources and productive capacity of these countries was significantly large.

But that glut was short-lived. Coinciding with the period of the emerging technological revolution in micro-computers and in gene technology which attracted capital to new fields where the rates of profit were likely to be substantial (Sivanandan, 1979), the 1980s saw significant increases in the cost of borrowing. As interest rates rose, debtor countries were suddenly faced with servicing the interest on loans which absorbed ever-greater proportions of export earnings. Debt had now become the central issue of 'concern' in development circles.

The Bretton Woods institutions, which, in the post-war period, had invested so heavily to ensure the resuscitation of economies of Europe, became the new commanders of Third World economies. A clutch of social and economic policies that came to be known as structural adjustment programmes were applied, in the spirit of universality, across the board. The social and political impact of these policies was to position the multilateral lending agencies (with the support of the bilateral aid agencies) so that they could determine both the goals of development and the means for achieving them. It legitimised their direct intervention in political decision-making processes, enabling them, for example, to set the levels of producer and consumer prices. These institutions literally determined the extent of involvement which the State should have in the social sector, and insisted on the State's imposing draconian economic and social measures which resulted in a rise in unemployment and the decline in real incomes of the majority (Campbell, 1989). The result was to transform and restructure the social basis of power in African countries, strengthening those forces or alliances that would be sympathetic to the continued hegemony of the multilaterals and of the multinationals.

These measures had the effect of exacerbating the divisions between the 'haves' and the 'have-nots', between those who, for political reasons or for reasons of patronage, received benefits and those who did not. And the old, discredited theories of 'trickle-down', now ardently promoted by the IMF and World Bank, were adopted as the only legitimate way of enjoying the fruits of independence. Popular dissatisfaction with government policies led in the 1980s to spontaneous demonstrations, burning of crops, wildcat strikes, and similar expressions of discontent. Universities were closed, demonstrations brutally suppressed, strikes declared illegal. Trade unions, student organisations, popular organisations, and political parties became the target of repressive legislation.

Such widespread opposition resulted in some rethinking by official aid agencies and the multilaterals about how to present the same economic and social programmes with a more 'human face' (Cornia *et al*,

1987). Significant volumes of funds were set aside, aimed at 'mitigating' the 'social dimensions of adjustment'. The aim of such programmes was to act as palliatives which might minimise the more glaring inequalities that their policies had perpetuated. Funds were made available to ensure that social services for the 'vulnerable' would be provided — but this time not by the State (which had after all been forced to 'retrench' away from the social sector) but by the ever-willing NGO sector. The availability of such funds for this sector was to have a profound impact on its very nature.

'When elephants fight, the grass gets trampled'

The material basis for the rise of conflicts in Africa had been laid. A popular movement which had once organised itself around the struggle for rights and justice had been demobilised either through repression or by redirecting its attention to the apparently neutral territory of 'development'. The process of democratisation of the colonial State had been limited to deracialisation of urban civil society, while the rural peasantry remained constricted within the structures of Native Authority, established under colonialism. The development process itself had become a source of accumulation and patronage. Structural adjustment programmes exacerbated social differentiation. As the pie got smaller, with the increasing debt crisis and the deteriorating terms of trade, so the State became more repressive. And, just as had happened in the era of the 1920s, in the rural areas numerous religious and quasi-religious organisations, sects and other such movements emerged as the source of social solidarity, some entirely based on ethnic membership, others more diverse. And in the urban centres, the only tolerated form of organisation became the criminal networks which rooted themselves in the peri-urban ghettos of Africa's cities.

With the collapse of the Berlin Wall, the credibility of movements offering an alternative ideology to the Thatcherite 'get-rich-quick-beggar-thy-neighbour' capitalism also collapsed. Opposition was no longer a function of alternative ideas or policies or about who could enhance development, but now an open and frank fight in the market-place for economic hegemony. The collapse of ideology led thus to the legitimisation of ruthless competition: competition that was, in the absence of legitimate mechanisms for constraint or credible State machinery able to mediate it, increasingly conducted by the most ruthless means, in some cases (such as Sierra Leone and Liberia) military. The distinction between social organisation for criminal activities and for political purposes became blurred. Civilians became increasingly caught in the crossfire, or even became the targets of either the armed opposition groups or the increasingly desperate State machinery. Arrest and imprisonment of political opponents, once a critical focus for international protest against the despotic State, had now become a less frequently used form of repression. Instead, disappearances, political killings, and extra-judicial executions were the order of the day (Amnesty International Dutch Section, 1994).

The late 1980s also saw the re-emergence of the mass movement in South Africa from its brutal crushing in the 1960s and 1970s. The South African economy was paralysed, as were its political institutions. All eyes were turned south: everyone expected an explosion, a social revolution that would shake the continent. Legitimisation of political opposition and deracialisation of civil society in South Africa was the cry of the international community, who saw it as the only way to prevent the threat of social upheavals. But if political opposition and the freedoms of civil society were to be legitimised in one part of the continent, why not elsewhere?

So, in the 1990s, the focus of attention of the international community was placed upon persuading African governments to permit political pluralism in the form of 'multi-partyism'. Democratisation of the structures of the State had not occurred, and was certainly no longer in the interest of the ruling elites. The State's role in the social sector had been effectively gelded in the process of structural adjustment, and its decisive role in determining economic policy had been appropriated by the multilateral institutions. What was there left to offer which might stave off the possibilities of social upheavals? Pluralism in the political arena seemed the only possibility. But, far from legitimising any struggle for basic rights or for greater accountability of the State and its structures, the result has been to bring into the public domain the seething divisions between sections of the ruling class competing for control of the State. With their constituencies usually in the rural areas, the inevitable consequence was to bring the explosive tensions of tribalism into the urban context.

If the development process has become concerned with who gets access to what, then civil war is but a continuation of that process by other, albeit more destructive, means.[6] Civil war has frequently become the inexorable outcome of the development process itself. In Sierra Leone, both the army and the 'rebels' are major actors in the mining industry. The war in Liberia has become a lucrative venture for illegal mining, drug trafficking, and money laundering. Angola's protracted war has helped Savimbi and some multinational corporations to extract diamonds from the country: in 1993 alone, Savimbi's rebel group pocketed US$250 million from the mining towns which it controls. The South African mining conglomerate De Beers has admitted to the illegal purchase of diamonds mined in Angola worth some US$500 million. In 1992 alone, money laundered from drugs in war-torn countries amounted to about US$856 million.

The conflict which took place in Rwanda in 1994, resulting in the massacre of a million people in less than nine months, was a human catastrophe of immense proportions. But its underlying causes are a tragic example of the consequences of the combination of the factors noted above. The collapse of the International Coffee Agreement had a devastating effect on more than 70 per cent of households in the country, and Rwandan farmers expressed their anger and frustration in 1992 by cutting down some 3,000 coffee trees. This exacerbated the tensions which resulted from the attempted invasion of the Rwandese Patriotic Front (RPF). The government read the political mood and understood that its legitimacy was being challenged. In desperation, it became more repressive, disseminating hate propaganda against the supposed 'enemy', the Tutsi, and encouraging systematic killings and violations against any whom they defined as being Tutsi or the allies of Tutsi. The defence component of the government's already over-stretched budget grew substantially, the size of the army being increased from a mere 5,000 to over 40,000 soldiers. That was the context in which the World Bank insisted on the implementation of its standard package of social and economic policies aimed at reducing public expenditure, introducing privatisation and retrenchment, and making people pay more for health care and education. The effect was to increase the burden on the majority of Rwandese, 85 per cent of whom were living below the poverty line. In the context of the disintegration of fragile political institutions, the political impasse within the government itself over the Arusha Accords, which proposed power-sharing with the RPF, anything could have triggered the conflict. And that indeed happened when the presidential plane was shot down in April 1994.[7]

NGOs and the depoliticisation of poverty

What, then, has been the role of the non-government development agencies in this turbulent history?

It was, for sure, the post-colonial State which actively suppressed popular struggles for rights, and redirected attention, with the support of multilateral and bilateral official aid agencies, to the politically safer terrain of 'development'. Development NGOs have, nevertheless, played a pivotal role in the processes which accompanied modernisation and led to the depoliticisation of poverty. Indeed, they have become such an integral component of the political economy of under-development that they are now part of a system which contributes to the reproduction of impoverishment.

Development NGOs will vehemently claim that their work in developing countries is neutral. This assumption of neutrality probably has its origins in the heroic work which NGOs have frequently performed in response to crises. Under such circumstances, NGOs have adopted the essential humanitarian principle that all those affected by disasters should be treated equally and receive assistance equally. Humanitarian responses should take no sides in conflicts. The problem arises when these same principles have been applied in non-critical conditions, such as those which prevail in 'development' programmes or in conditions of prolonged crises, especially where, for example as in Somalia, the State itself has long ago collapsed. Why should that be so?

One of the most important roles which the State performs in any society is to guarantee the conditions for the reproduction of those social relations that enable the ruling class to continue to rule. If the State fails in that essential function, then the future of the ruling class itself is threatened. The new ruling classes of post-colonial Africa soon learned the import-ance of that — and those who were slow to learn were quickly swept aside by *coups d'état* or civil war.

'Development' (or the political economy, more precisely) as defined by the ruling class, was the process which would be used to ensure the reproduction of the required social relations that reproduced impoverishment and injustice for the many, and rapid accumulation of wealth for the few. But is there a space wherein NGOs can carry out their charitable work without 'taking sides' in the process of reproduction of these social relations? I believe not. The fact is that many NGOs have, unwittingly or willingly, inserted themselves over the last few decades as part of the very infrastructure of the political economy that reproduces the unequal social relations of post-colonial Africa.[8]

This has not always been the case. In the period of anti-colonial struggles, many NGOs actively participated in solidarity movements or supported directly anti-imperialist organisations. Their participation in such activities was informed by their (albeit intuitive) understanding that existing social relations of colonial rule needed to be overthrown. The same was also true of those NGOs who participated in the anti-apartheid movement or supported the work of the Mass Democratic Movement in South Africa prior to the release of Nelson Mandela.

But with independence, the dilemma which NGOs faced (and one which many have faced in South Africa recently) was a difficult one: the *ancien régime* had been overthrown. The conditions for its reproduction had been destroyed. Surely the role of NGOs should now be to participate in the process of ensuring the reproduction of the new regime, the new social order? And surely, the answer to that should be in the affirmative? But only, I believe, insofar as the new social order was not intent on the perpetuation of old injustices or on the creation of new forms of exploitation.

But how were NGOs to know how things would turn out in the future? Caught in the traumatic upheavals which characterised the victory over colonialism (and against apartheid), it was easy to become romantic and blinkered by one's own enthusiasm. It was hardly surprising that many NGOs became closely involved in 'bringing development to the people' in the newly independent countries. But the real problem was that the dominant discourse on development was framed not in the language of rights and justice, but in the vocabulary of charity, technical expertise, neutrality, and a deep paternalism (albeit accompanied by the rhetoric of participatory development) which was its syntax.[9]

This was a period in which the involvement of Northern NGOs in Africa grew dramatically. The number of international NGOs operating in Kenya, for example, increased almost three-fold to 134 during the period 1978 to 1988 (Osodo and Matsvai, 1998). Most of the Northern NGOs preoccupied themselves with 'projects' which would benefit 'the poor' and whose main purpose was to bring 'development'. This process took place in the context of the efforts of the new regimes seeking to demobilise the popular movement. Official sanction for their projects was provided not just from central government, but also from local authority structures in the rural areas — the Native Authority which had been formerly established by colonial rule and subsequently reinforced by the new State. Sanction from these authorities served to reinforce their own legitimacy.

As repression of those who were seen to be political opponents became a feature of the new State, seeking to centralise its control, many NGOs chose to remain silent about that creeping repression. Protest against repression of political opponents was largely left to (Northern) human-rights organisations. The dilemma faced by NGOs was that such protests could jeopardise the grants which they received from the official aid agencies (who, certainly until the mid-1980s, rarely sought to comment on the excesses of African governments). NGOs, especially the Northern ones, also feared that protest could jeopardise their own relationship with the national government to whom they were beholden for a range of privileges (such as exemptions from tax or duty). There was little point, some argued, in making a fuss, since 'it would only be the poor who would suffer as a result'.

Over time, their role evolved from their anti-colonial activities until they became one of the central actors in the process of development itself. NGOs, especially those from the North, began to insert themselves as vital cogs in the new political economy, the vehicles through which an increasing proportion of development programmes were implemented. They were armed with manuals and all the technical expertise for focusing the attention of 'the poor' on coping with the present, rather than seeking justice for past crimes against them. Like their missionary predecessors, they offered the poor blessings in the future (albeit on earth rather than in heaven). Most remained unconscious of the fact that it was the very system which reproduced the impoverishment, injustice and conflict which the NGOs claimed it was their mission was to abolish.

Their insertion was effectively completed in the era of structural adjustment. This era witnessed the retrenching State absolving itself of the responsibility for providing social services, while investing in the growth of the private sector. The number of NGOs, the private entrepreneurs *par excellence* in the public sector, once again expanded (with the encouragement of lavish sums available from aid agencies) in their new role as sub-contractors to the official aid agencies for the delivery of social services. They became the 'human face' of adjustment itself. And as aid budgets in the North declined (ACTIONAID *et al*, 1997), and as greater volumes of funds were made available through direct funding (INTRAC, 1998), so Northern NGOs sought to accommodate to the new environment by legally registering themselves as 'local NGOs', the better to tap the vast sums available locally. One of the effects of this has been to transform the Northern NGO from being a donor/supporter of local NGOs to becoming a direct competitor for aid funds in the local market. Meanwhile, hundreds of local NGOs were established whose sole purpose was to become the sub-contractors for the provision of social services which would mitigate the effects of adjustment for the 'vulnerable' or 'poorest of the poor'.

The field of development had become 'big business', requiring an entourage of experts committed to the goal of making the unsustainable sustainable. By the 1990s, many of the larger Northern NGOs had begun a process of recomposition ('restructuring'). This process led to the establishment of formations similar to the transnational corporation of the private sector. New forms of multinational structures and an internationalisation of the 'brand' have become the features of that recomposition, mimicking in the NGO sectors the forms of globalisation which GATT and the World Trade Organisation (WTO) legitimised in the private. The multinational or transnational NGO came into existence with the sole purpose of effectively delivering aid with the forms of 'professionalism' required by the official aid agencies. It raised funds on the basis of the global brand-name, whose image had become well established among these agencies and multinational corporations as the guarantor or fstability and reliability — the trustworthy depoliticiser of poverty.

In the process, concerns about the rights of the vast majority of the population, their search for freedom from oppression and exploitation, had become peripheral. Northern NGOs in particular were now more preoccupied with fundraising on the basis of portraying Africans as the subject of pity, people whose plight would be relieved through acts of charity. In the region, this approach served to foster demobilisation and disillusion. In the North, the public's prejudices were reinforced: Africans were perceived as hopeless, as mere victims of endless civil war, and as passive recipients of Northern charity.[10]

But was it inevitable that NGOs would become so thoroughly integrated into the political economy of Africa as to become partners in the reproduction of social relations which give rise to impoverishment and conflict? Is it inevitable that they will continue to do so? The cynical view is perhaps that the development NGO has long ago developed a vested interest in the continued reproduction of such social relations, and that they will 'do better the less stable the world becomes ... [because] ... finance will become increasingly available to agencies who can deliver "stabilising" social services' (Fowler, 1997, p. 229)

I believe that the option exists for NGOs to choose otherwise, if they recognise that there is no 'neutral' ground, no 'no-man's land' in the process of development. Those who believe there is neutral territory frequently become prey to the agendas of other social forces. They would do well to reflect on the following excerpt from a USAID review quoted by Nelson Mandela in his recent report to the ANC Congress:

Two-thirds of [US]AID's funding ... is used to fund AID-dependent NGOs ... The Old 'struggle NGOs' have been redesignated by AID as 'civil service organisations' (or CSOs). AID now funds CSOs to 'monitor public policy, provide information, and advocate policy alternatives' and to serve as 'sentinels, brokers and arbiters for the public will.' The purpose of AID's funding is to enable these CSOs to 'function as effective policy advocacy groups' and 'to lobby'... Through its NGOs, AID intends to play a key role in domestic policy concerning the most difficult, controversial issues of national politics. AID's political agenda is ambitious and extensive.

(Munson and Christenson, 1996)

The choice is thus a stark one: either play the role (unwittingly or otherwise) of reinforcing those social relations that reproduce impoverishment, injustice, and conflict. Or make the choice to play a positive role in supporting those processes in society that will overturn those social relations.

If NGOs are to play a positive role, then it will need to be based on two premises: solidarity and rights. Solidarity is not about fighting other people's battles. It is about establishing co-operation between different constituencies on the basis on mutual self-respect and concerns about the injustices suffered by each. It is about taking sides in the face of injustice or the processes which reproduce injustice. It is not built on sympathy or charity or the portrayal of others as objects of pity. It is not about fundraising to run your projects overseas, but raising funds which others can use to fight their own battles. It is about taking actions within one's own terrain which will enhance the capacity of others to succeed in their fight against injustice.

The issue of rights might appear to be more complex. The ways in which the concept of rights has been articulated and practised in the North reflect the specificity of historical experiences of struggles for rights that were intrinsic to those societies, and whose foundations lay in the bourgeois revolutions of Europe. That is at it should be. Problems arise when it is assumed that those experiences are sufficient for proclaiming their universality. This is not to say that the rights that are articulated in the UDHR and other covenants are not relevant to Africa. Clearly they have universal significance. Rather, it is to assert that as yet they do not protect the totality of all those human values that deserve protection. For example, it was partly in recognition of the limitations of existing human-rights instruments that the African Charter on Human and Peoples' Rights was established in 1986, the only regional human-rights agreement that asserts the collective rights of people as well as environmental rights. But proclamations about the universality of the Northern concepts of rights lead only to sterile rhetoric. The issue is not that rights need to be presented, like a washing powder, with more relevant symbols from Africa's cultural experiences (Penna and Campbell, 1998). That misses the point. Rather, rights should not be theorised as legal rights ' … which implies both a static and an absolutist paradigm, in the sense of an entitlement or claim, but a means of struggle. In that sense it is akin to righteousness rather than right. Seen as a means of struggle, "right" is therefore not a standard granted as charity from above, but a standard-bearer around which people rally for the struggle from below' (Shivji, 1989: 71)

The field of human rights has recently found much favour among the official aid agencies. The latter regard support for rights as a means for 'improving good governance', 'promoting democracy', and 'strengthening civil society' (INTRAC, 1998). Unfortunately the focus of many human-rights organisations has been almost exclusively on agitations to claim civil and political rights. Their work remains focused primarily on the urban areas, leaving unchallenged the structures of power which continue to hold hegemony in the name of customary power. As Mamdani points out, '… So long as rural power is organised as a fused authority that denies rights in the name of enforcing custom, civil society will remain an urban phenomenon' (Mamdani, 1996: 293). And so long as the opposition and the movement for rights do not seek to dismantle the rural structures of power, the dangerous tensions inherent in the bifurcated state in Africa will continue.

In the anti-colonial period, many NGOs demonstrated their capacity to express solidarity and to focus their prime attention on supporting the struggle of African peoples for rights. If that capacity has not already been exhausted, I believe there is a need to return to that tradition. The alternative is to stand impotent and bewildered, as NGOs did when the genocide erupted in Rwanda: impotent because they did not understand what could have been done, and bewildered because of their unease that the processes of development in Africa, of which NGOs have become such an integral part, themselves gave rise to the conflicts and to the terrors of genocide.

The slogan which gave rise to the UDHR was 'never again' to genocide. There is a bitter irony in the fact that, when it happened again in Africa, the signatories to that proclamation were silent or unwilling to act. Rwanda has demonstrated that the proclamation was deficient. It remains for popular movements and organisations of Africa to rebuild the tradition based on its own experiences which can guarantee the conditions in which genocide will never again be possible. This will be no easy task. Whether or not development NGOs can participate in that process will depend largely on whether they continue to define their role as part of the political economy of a form of development that breeds and sustains inequalities and conflicts, or whether they rally to the standard of solidarity and rights. The choice is theirs.

Notes

1 In South Africa, similar forms of organisation were seen during the same period until the movement was brutally crushed, only to re-emerge (albeit in other forms) in the late 1970s. The processes which characterised South Africa in the lead-up to the first elections and the gradual transformation of the struggle for rights into the realm of 'development' have uncanny similarities to what happened in the rest of the continent.

2 Let us be frank: for the rural and peri-urban populations, the quality of services had little to distinguish them, apart from their deracialised form, from those provided to the black populations under apartheid.

3 These achievements challenge the current, largely ideologically motivated, caricature of the State as being 'inefficient' and unable to deliver effective services. Certainly the post-independence State has been a largely unaccountable one, but the alternative structures which have been enforced by the multilateral lending agencies have not been any less accountable to the people.

4 The identification of the victims as the problem is not unique to the field of development. For years, successive British governments (Tory and Labour) have defined the victims of racism, black people in Britain, as the problem, the solution to which was to introduce immigration controls and repressive police controls in the ghettos to which blacks had been confined. See Sivanandan, 1983.

5 As more and more African states achieved independence, the UDHR has been endorsed by the new governments as a set of principles underpinning their constitutions. The bulk of subsequent international human-rights standards have been adopted with the participation of African States. Nevertheless, virtually every single State has been guilty of repeated violations of human rights, few being willing to do more than make paper modifications of their national legislation in line with the treaties or conventions to which they are signatories.

6 Mamdani (1996) goes further. He characterises tribalism as 'civil war', because the 'notion of civil war is a continuum along which muted tensions coexist long before they break out into open confrontation' (p. 292).

7 Some of the ideas presented in this section were first developed in a

paper presented by Pierre Sane and myself, entitled 'Africa: Development, Conflict and Human Rights', at the Twentieth Anniversary of North-South Institute, Ottawa, 1996.

8 There are parallels to be drawn between the claims of neutrality and charity of some NGOs today and similar claims made by their missionary predecessors in pre-independence Africa.

9 Interestingly enough, during this period the Northern NGOs established the same racial division of labour that had once characterised the missionary outposts and the colonial State. The white expatriate, the technical expert, was usually the head of the local office. Militant at home about parity in salary scales within their home organisations, the Northern NGO in Africa came armed with a baggage full of reasons (usually transported in a four-wheel-drive vehicle) why local staff should not be paid at the same rates.

10 The films shown on television about Africa, produced by Comic Relief, a highly successful fundraising organisation in the UK, epitomised this paternalistic approach. One of the founders of that organisation expressed once his frustrations that the disability lobby in the UK had become so militant that it was no longer possible for Comic Relief to make similar films about disability in the UK! It is perhaps the physical distance from their 'beneficiaries' which allows the development NGOs to get away with their paternalism with such impunity.

References

ACTIONAID et al: *The Reality of Aid 1996*, London: Earthscan, 1997.

Amnesty International Dutch Section (1994) *Disappearances and Political Killings: Human Rights Crisis of the 1990s*, Amsterdam: Amnesty International.

Barratt Brown, M. (1995) *Africa's Choices*, London: Penguin Books.

Campbell, B. (1989) 'Indebtedness in Africa: consequence, cause or symptom of the crisis?' in Bade Onimode (ed.): *The IMF, the World Bank and the African Debt: The Social and Political Impact*, London: Zed Books, pp. 17–30.

Cornia, G., R. Jolly and F. Stewart (1987) *Adjustment with a Human Face*, Oxford: Clarendon Press.

Fowler, A. (1997) *Striking a Balance*, London: Earthscan.

INTRAC (1998) *Direct Funding*, Oxford: INTRAC (in press).

Mamdani, M. (1996) *Citizen and Subject: Contemporary Africa and the Legacy of Late Colonialism*, London: James Currey.

Mandel, E. (1975) *Late Capitalism*, New Left Books.

Munson, Lester and Phillip Christenson (1996) 'Review of US Aid Program in South Africa', 5 November 1996; cited in N. Mandela (1997) 'Report by the President of the ANC, Nelson Mandela, to the 50th National Conference of the African National Congress', *Mafikeng*, 16 December 1997.

Osodo, P. and S. Matsvai (1998) *Partners or Contractors: The Relationship between Official Agencies and NGOs — Kenya and Zimbabwe*, INTRAC Occasional Papers No. 10, Oxford: INTRAC.

Payer, C. (1989) 'Causes of the debt crisis', in Bade Onimode (ed.) *The IMF, the World Bank and the African Debt: The Social and Political Impact*, London: Zed Books, pp. 7–16.

Penna, D. R. and P. J. Campbell (1998) 'Human rights and culture: beyond universality and relativism', *Third World Quarterly* 19/1, pp. 7–27.

Rodney, W. (1976) *How Europe Underdeveloped Africa*, Dar es Salaam: Tanzania Publishing House.

Sivanandan, A. (1979) 'Imperialism and disorganic development in the silicon age', *Race and Class* XXIV (2).

Sivanandan, A. (1983) *A Different Hunger: Writings on Black Resistance*, London: Pluto Press, pp 3–54.

Shivji, I. (1989) *The Concept of Human Rights in Africa*, London: CODESRIA.

United Nations Development Programme (1997) *Human Development Report 1997*, Oxford: Oxford University Press.

World Bank (1981) *World Development Report 1980*, Washington: World Bank.

■ **Firoze Manji,** *a Kenyan, was formerly Director of Amnesty International's Africa Programme. He has worked for a number of international agencies and has extensive experience of living and working in Africa.*

The humanitarian responsibilities of the UN Security Council: ensuring the security of the people[1]

Juan Somavía

Introduction

The question of the humanitarian responsibilities of the Security Council is for me a natural sequel to the 1995 World Summit for Social Development, of which I was Chair. It concerns the challenge of putting people at the centre of development and international cooperation, this time in a different sphere of action within the United Nations (UN). Humanitarian tasks and development objectives continually intersect and reinforce each other. They are not sequential, but different dimensions of an integrated understanding of how to promote the security of people. A comprehensive and integrated view of these questions goes far beyond the scope of this paper. Rather, I shall limit myself to matters which the Council should deal with more urgently.

Conceptual framework, definitions, and key issues

The UN Charter confers on the Security Council prime responsibility for the maintenance of international peace and security. Until recently, this has been understood basically to mean disputes among States with international consequences. Yet these two concepts — peace and security, the very conceptual foundations for the UN's mission — are undergoing a radical change in the way they are perceived.

Peace, as we know, is much more than the mere absence of war. It has come to mean harmony within as well as among nations. Countries which are not actively 'at war' with other countries are not necessarily at peace with themselves. In an era when individual people and communities struggle to hold their own against seemingly insuperable odds, peace increasingly means more than the absence of threats and discrimination. It means freedom from fear and want. For people everywhere, the heart of peace is peace within our own hearts, within our families, our schools, our work-places, our communities. Peace has acquired a human dimension far larger than the original State-centred notion of the UN Charter; and we have learned that its absence at the local and national levels can have multiple international implications.

The concept of security is also evolving. Today it means inclusion, cohesion, and integration — a sense of belonging to a society and a prevailing order within and among nations that is predicated on fairness and respect for differences and human dignity. The only legitimate (and lasting) security is security rooted in the well-being of people. We have all observed that you can have a secure State — in the traditional sense — full of insecure people who face poverty, destitution, and threats to their integrity. The security of people has thus emerged as a complementary and distinct notion from that of the security of the State.

Another important evolution has been the growing presence on the Security Council agenda of internal conflicts in which the 'parties to a dispute' are not sovereign States but rather groups or factions within a State, sometimes mere warlords, most of whom do not represent an entity with the attributes of a State as defined by the traditional norms of international law.

The first ten years of the Security Council's activities were marked by State conflicts arising out of Cold War situations, the initial tensions of the decolonisation process, threats of external aggression, and traditional frontier-disputes among countries. In each, the humanitarian dimension existed but was not a central feature of the dispute.

In the last ten years, by contrast, the agenda of the Security Council has been fraught with civil wars in which the threat to civilian lives looms paramount. Suffice it to mention Namibia, Cambodia, El Salvador, Guatemala, Afghanistan, Georgia, Angola, Mozambique, and Liberia—as well as Somalia, Rwanda, Burundi, and the Former Yugoslavia—to know what we mean. In these types of conflict, it is increasingly civilians (unarmed and unprotected) who are the principal victims. During World War I, five per cent of all casualties were civilians; in Cambodia and Rwanda, almost 95 per cent were.

Further, it is understood that the Security Council operates under the aegis of the basic principles of international law, a central tenet of which is non-interference in the internal affairs of States. Yet, if the Council is to be effective in promoting solutions and agreements to end this type of conflict, it inevitably becomes deeply involved in the internal affairs of the society in question. Moreover, if the crisis is serious enough, there are, understandably, strong public calls for the Council to 'do something' to prevent death and destruction.

Recently, the Security Council has repeatedly been told: 'Look at the horrible tragedies that are going on in the world. Do something about them!' But the whole tradition of diplomacy leads elsewhere. It is difficult to apply classical diplomacy to these new conflicts.

The evolution of the concepts of peace and security — against the backdrop of mainly internal conflicts posing grave threats to civilians, and an international public opinion that demands action — raises new issues and requires the Council to re-examine the appropriateness and effectiveness of existing instruments and traditional diplomatic courses of action. This suggests that a stronger link must develop between the UN, the Security Council, and organisations like Oxfam which are on the ground, doing humanitarian work, touching those societies, looking into the eyes of the people in danger, learning who they are and what is going on, who the factions are, and what relations people have with their leaders — much of which never gets to the table of the Security Council.

A window on civil society

Maintaining peace and security must take into account the underlying causes of conflict, often development-related, as well as the expressions of power-struggles among leaders and factions. The nature of preventive diplomacy, conflict-resolution, peace-making, and peace-building, however, is still too State-centric. Together, governments and civil society must evolve a more dynamic concept and praxis, within which non-government actors play a key role. The notion of what some of us call 'preventive development' is crucial: conflicts often have their origins in socio-economic conditions, but are too often dealt with as if they were exclusively political problems. We need to link analysis of the development causes to the actual political processes under way. We can also build upon the lessons learned from experiences of conflict-resolution efforts at the inter-personal level and within divided communities, which are sometimes more relevant than classical dispute-resolution tools.

The tendency to think of peace and security in State-centric terms also fails to take into account the multiple social and economic factors which underpin the security of people, or the vital need to safeguard and support individual actors in civil society, whose energy and mutual confidence are essential to maintaining peace and security in the long term. A critical feature of the last decade is the civil-society movement, which is burgeoning all over the world. The impact of non-government actors of immense variety — representatives of trade unions, churches, voluntary groups, and grassroots organisations—has been tremendous. It is now generally acknowledged that together they have helped to shape our contemporary definitions of sustainable development, population, gender, and human rights, and in their characteristically practical style they have pushed governments to develop the means to translate these concepts into action.

But they are also centrally involved in humanitarian relief, thus helping to increase the chances of conflict-resolution. The essentially internal dimensions of contemporary crisis — and the increasingly central role played by non-government actors in forging a culture of sustainable peace — have brought NGOs and other non-government actors much closer than before to the analysis and action of international political affairs. This is happening *de facto*, but, in my view, it is insufficiently recognised by the Security Council. Consequently, the experience of humanitarian organisations is being under-used.

The Council's method of work and mandate are sufficiently broad to incorporate, in an appropriate way, inputs from civil-society organisations within its scope of operations. However, these elements are less than broadly interpreted — and much less than flexibly applied. Indeed, while acknowledging the highly sensitive nature of the Council's work, more widespread consultation and transparent decision-making is necessary, not only to enhance accountability *vis à vis* the General Assembly, member governments, and public opinion, but also to provide a broader basis of information, experience, and professional advice for its decision-making.

Given that so many non-government actors are now involved in assisting, safeguarding, and enhancing the security of people threatened by conflict, it is only logical that their role should be fully acknowledged and that they should be enabled (safely and successfully) to make their specific humanitarian contribution. It is thus in practical terms that I wish to consider the Security Council here.

I am convinced that the Security Council itself could be better organised to this end. Here, I would refer to several provocative suggestions set forth in an excellent report entitled *The International*

Response to Conflict and Genocide: Lessons from the Rwandan Experience.[2] It contains a number of practical suggestions, highlighting a re-invigorated role for the Department of Humanitarian Affairs (DHA), as well as the role of regional organisations and NGOs, the military, the judiciary, and the media, which are well worth considering.

I would add that what the Council truly needs is an additional mechanism to raise the political profile of humanitarian coordination, to put it on a par with military coordination. Let me offer a practical example: Chile and other countries have advocated that troop-contributing nations be directly privy to Security Council deliberations over where and how their soldiers will be deployed in peace-keeping operations. A special provision for consultation has been approved for this purpose.[3]

Similarly, there should be regular consultations with external actors who have a unique and often first-hand perspective on the specificity of a given conflict, and on where and how humanitarian operations can most safely and productively be undertaken. Such background information and exchange would enhance the decision-making capacity of the Council. However, I should interject a note of caution, to urge that the autonomy and independence of humanitarian work must be safe-guarded in all circumstances.

The consultations could evolve from existing contacts with humanitarian NGOs undertaken by the DHA, and have an informal character.

Security of humanitarian relief

What forms of protection exist for the non-government community in situations of armed conflict and in complex emergencies threatening the lives of large numbers of civilians?

As we have seen, with the end of the Cold War, the UN has become increasingly involved in resolving conflict within States in crisis. Calls upon the UN to take a proactive role in responding to complex emergencies have increased apace. In this context, the safety on the ground of UN and non-UN personnel alike has become a pressing issue. Staff of Oxfam and other NGOs have fallen victim to brutal attacks and harassment over the past year. In addition to the Oxfam worker recently killed in Angola, three Red Cross workers were murdered in Burundi in June 1996. The irony is that, while their loss was mourned among many in the non-government community, it provoked nowhere near the response which the loss of uniformed military personnel has elicited in connection with UN peace-building operations elsewhere.

Indeed, sometimes governments appear more willing to sacrifice the lives of relief workers than they do those of their own troops. The former serve out of the conviction that their presence builds peace; the latter accept participation in the dangers of conflict as part of their terms of service. Yet it is often non-uniformed relief and development workers who are on the front lines of conflicts in which some governments are reluctant to commit their own troops.

This situation is quite incredible: one group are the professionals — instructed and trained to deal with danger — and yet, for various internal political reasons, governments are unwilling to place them at risk. The other group are there out of conviction, out of their beliefs and values, and are prepared to face the dangers and difficulties. Yet relief and development workers operate with far fewer resources or forms of protection, and stay long after the active fighting has ceased — often remaining until security in its fullest sense is assured, or until it is patently impossible for them to stay.

Some would argue that relief and development workers have become *de facto* advance troops in conflicts where States parties have no real political intent or practical means to guarantee their safety — let alone to achieve peace. Others allege that the political and humanitarian dimensions of complex emergencies are poorly understood, and that lack of coherent assessment, priority-setting, and field operations on the part of the international community not only prolongs the agony of people living in countries in crisis, but puts at risk those trying to help them.

The Security Council itself, in light of the tragedies which have unfolded over the course of the past five years in Afghanistan, Angola, Bosnia, Burundi, Georgia, Haiti, Lebanon, Liberia, Rwanda, Somalia and elsewhere, has begun to refer explicitly in its decisions to the role of non-government humanitarian actors in peace-building and emergency situations. A recent statement on Somalia by the President of the Security Council reflects this trend: 'The Security Council considers the *uninterrupted delivery of humanitarian assistance to be a crucial factor in the overall security and stability of Somalia'*. I consider this to be a very significant political recognition of the role that humanitarian agencies are playing in situations of conflict.

Humanitarian concerns have indeed become central to the calculus of whether and how the UN's continued (official) presence in a country can advance the peace-building process. On Liberia, statements by the President have been equally direct, noting that, as of early April 1996, 'factional fighting, the harassment and abuse of the civilian population and humanitarian and relief workers' had increased to the point that the country's political leaders 'risk[ed] losing the support of the international community'.[4]

The challenge is to develop a series of inter-locking legal and logical safeguards that are shored up by the political will of countries to enforce them, and operationalised through a coherent UN system which functions in tandem with regional, national, and local institutions.

The ultimate responsibility for peace, however, rests with those in power in a given country. I deliberately avoid the use of the word 'government', for often those in power have not necessarily been elected, nor do they conduct themselves with any sense of civic obligation towards majority rule, or the capacity to govern effectively. Their claim to legitimacy often rests on nothing more than having gained physical control of the capital city and seat of government through force. Pressure can nonetheless be brought to bear upon those in power: pressure not only to resolve a conflict, but to respect the humanity of individuals engaged in building the foundations of a sustainable peace, whether formally in partnership with the UN or independently.

I also believe that the Council should consider the compelling issue of strengthened legal provisions for the protection of humanitarian workers. This is an extremely complex issue, but we know that law is only as vigorous as its application. We must address the challenges of implementing international humanitarian law (IHL). Discourse on this subject has occupied policy-makers and academics for the better part of the past century; however, I raise it here because of the compelling nature — indeed, the urgency — of the subject, given the proliferation of highly complex conflicts in which the principal disputants appear increasingly dismissive of these fundamental anchors of global order. Given, too, the multiplicity of agents involved in relief work, we must find new ways to strengthen the legal safeguards available.

There is a *lacuna* in international law today, where non-government workers act more or less autonomously in a conflict situation, unprotected. All there is at present is a UN convention which safeguards those who perform humanitarian work done in agreement with and under the aegis of the framework of the UN—but no-one else.

Oxfam and others in civil society might press for the creation of a separate convention which *explicitly* protects non-government personnel and others affiliated to UN relief efforts — whether or not they operate directly under the umbrella of UN control. I believe we should explore what kinds of protection and enforcement should be guaranteed by such a convention. Who would adjudicate it? and how could reporting and related enforcement be expeditiously and effectively ensured? What can be done to strengthen the mechanisms for the implementation of IHL? As we know, signatory States are enjoined, under the Geneva Conventions, to respect core provisions concerning the protection of the sick and wounded, prisoners of war, and civilians. Through a mix of injunctions and prohibitions on contracting parties, the Conventions seek to protect 'undefended localities' from attack, while at the same time forbidding murder, torture, collective punishment, and hostage-taking— all of which are woefully common in contemporary conflict.

However, as argued in Oxfam's September 1995 position paper prepared on the occasion of the UN's 50th Anniversary (provocatively entitled 'A Failed Opportunity?'),

> international humanitarian law, including the Geneva Conventions, [is] upheld in very few modern conflicts ... the debate about addressing the problem concentrates more on limiting the rights of States, rather than seeking to enforce the rights of individuals.

This is a very apt assessment.

The fact that sanctions on States in breach of the Conventions are extremely problematic has led some to suggest that individual reprisals are preferable. The recent tribunals established to address war crimes in the Former Yugoslavia and genocide in Rwanda, respectively, offer a useful example of mechanisms for punishing individuals who violate the rules of IHL. It is encouraging to recognise that people throughout the world are saying: 'enough — an end to impunity'. Think about the difference in our collective consciousness from the days of Pol Pot—and the genocide of millions in Cambodia, where there were no tribunals — and our efforts today.

However, the operational (and financial) challenges faced by these tribunals is sobering. And even if an individual approach is pursued, there are blank spots in the Geneva Conventions; for example, they do not cover 'gender crimes', like large-scale and individual rape as a method of torture and intimidation.

Herein, States can and must exercise their responsibility to ensure that IHL is respected and rights observed. The difficulty in bringing to justice the Serbian leaders Karadzic and Mladic, together with less visible Croatian and Bosnian personnel indicted, is a clear example: a painful reminder of the separation between the notion that becomes law, and the capacity to make the law become reality.

Above all, the importance of international NGO contributions to humanitarian efforts cannot and should not be allowed to substitute for political will on the part of governments. Neither reforms in the organisation of the Security Council and its consultative mechanisms, nor the creation of additional legal protections for humanitarian workers, can substitute for what governments and governments alone can do. Governments have the responsibility to use their political clout, military capability, financial means, and diplomatic capacity to help to solve these conflicts. The increasing role of humanitarian agencies is no excuse for their inaction. Highlighting the role of NGOs should serve to *reinforce* the responslblllty of governments in this field.

Making sanctions more humane and effective

How does the international community engage itself in addressing the consequences of sanctions for civilians? The consequences of conflict include large numbers of refugees and displaced persons; famines and shortages of food and water; prisoners of war and combatants missing in action; violations of human rights; genocide and gross breaches of international humanitarian law; and also the effects of economic sanctions.

With limitations, there exist international mechanisms to address some of these consequences: among them, the office of the UN High Commissioner for Refugees (UNHCR); the World Food Programme (WFP); the Geneva Conventions; the human-rights mechanisms of the UN system; and the international criminal tribunals for the Former Yugoslavia and Rwanda, as well as the Commission of Inquiry for Burundi.

By contrast, economic sanctions are a rough, blunt, and extremely unsophisticated measure. We need to develop policies and instruments to make sanctions more humane and, at the same time, more effective. Both the underlying concepts and the implementation mechanisms need to be reviewed, taking into account the fact that in some instances (such as in South Africa and Burundi) some local and regional actors themselves felt that sanctions were necessary.

I am not asserting that sanctions are *a priori* illegitimate. On the contrary, the foundation of every national legal system is the notion that breaking the law incurs a sanction. So it should be for the international system. There is no quarrel over the principle; that is why the Security Council has the authority to apply sanctions. The problem lies in the effects of applying these measures in practice.

A close read of the UN Charter reveals that sanctions essentially aim to condition the behaviour of a State which poses a threat to international peace and security — not to punish or otherwise exact retribution,[5] and even less to contribute to a crisis for the civilians of the nation affected. Sanctions must be based on fundamental respect for human dignity. Indeed, the aim is to bring a State that has violated justice into good working relations within the community of nations, to cite one thoughtful interpretation.[6]

Chapter VII of the Charter thus empowers the Security Council to use both military and non-military measures to maintain or restore international peace and security. Article 41 outlines the nature of non-military sanctions — specifying that the Council may call upon the member States of the UN to apply 'complete or partial interruption of economic relations and of rail, sea, air, postal, telegraphic, radio, and other means of communications, and the severance of diplomatic relations' in order to give effect to the Council's decision.

Yet the conceptual basis for sanctions is flawed, in that they are premised on implicitly democratic assumptions, but are normally leveraged upon more or less authoritarian regimes. It is assumed that the people in a targeted country who will first feel the negative impact of sanctions are sufficiently empowered to pressure the government to cease the aggression or offence which triggered the sanctions. This is seldom the case in an undemocratic setting. Moreover, Johan Galtung and others have argued that sanctions can disempower and weaken the opponents of a regime by offering a common, external enemy against which to rally collective opposition — thereby distracting attention from domestic problems.[7]

Sanctions normally fail to affect the lives of the leaders of such regimes; instead they hit the most vulnerable the hardest; in that sense, they are highly disproportionate. While 'humanitarian exceptions' can be made to allow the targeted country to receive or purchase medical or food supplies, for example, there are no set guidelines for regulating when and how humanitarian assistance is to be provided.

Iraq is a good case in point. After the Gulf War, wide-ranging sanctions were applied by the Security Council in 1991, including a humanitarian exception.[8] At the same time, a trade embargo was imposed. Iraq's means to make use of the exception became severely limited, and the government did not give priority to food and medicine in the use of its internal resources. When data from FAO, WHO, UNICEF, and private organisations began to reveal the terrible consequences for ordinary people, the Security Council approved in 1995 the now well-known Resolution 986, which permitted the sale of oil for food and medicine. In 1996, an agreement was reached between the Secretary-General and the Government of Iraq to implement this resolution.

This situation begs the obvious question: did the Security Council have to wait until 1995, and Iraq postpone its response until 1996, to alleviate the suffering of the more destitute of the Iraqi people? Shouldn't the 'oil for food and medicine' agreement have been a part of the initial sanctions resolution? Were all the deaths and infirmities necessary? What political purpose of the international community was served by them?

Furthermore, practice has shown that the targeted government will prefer to use any resources available to prop up its own power through military spending, and disbursements for the elites and the groups and factions that give it political support. The well-being of the general population (which, under authoritarian conditions, has little ability to react) has not proven to be accorded priority. Iraq is a textbook case. So is the Former Yugoslavia, which chose to use existing resources to wage a regional war and support its regime and its Serbian allies, while under-reporting the impact of sanctions on civilians, so as to avoid international pressure and scrutiny.

Ultimately, sanctions as currently practised produce large-scale insecurity for ordinary people, the opposite of their intended effect. The Security Council should address the issue promptly. The principal objective would be to make sanctions regimes both more effective and more humane.[9]

As a first step, the Council should adopt a resolution approving a set of humanitarian norms, standards, and practices applicable to any sanctions regime to be established in the future. Such guidelines should bear in mind that humanitarian requirements may differ according to the stage of development, geography, natural resources, and other features of the affected society.

A clear position by the Council would have a number of advantages. It would avoid double standards and be a practical response to a real problem which the Council was facing, and should be flexible enough to encompass different realities. Its end result would be to ensure that the Security Council would act in such a way as to ensure that civilians did not suffer the consequences of sanctions regimes. This approach goes much further than the General Assembly's normal method of dealing with the matter (namely, by stating that 'unintended adverse side effects on the civilian population should be minimised' by appropriate humanitarian exceptions).[10]

It is disingenuous to talk of 'unintended side effects', when everybody knows that the sector most affected by sanctions, as presently applied, is precisely the civilian population. There is nothing surprising or unintended about it. That is how economic sanctions actually operate in practice. We are all perfectly aware of it.

A clear position by the Security Council could address or provide a framework that would achieve the following:

■ *Establish that the purpose of sanctions is to modify the behaviour of any party, not only a government, that is threatening international peace and security*, not to punish or otherwise exact retribution and even less to impose hardships on the population at large. Sanctions regimes should be commensurate with these objectives, and proportionality should be a guiding criterion.

■ *Ensure that sanctions are primarily addressed to the leaders in conflict*, by targeting them on the military and civilian structures which support the regime, and on the factions, groups, and warlords that are parties to a civil-war type of conflict. The impact of sanctions could be shifted from the people at large to the leaders in particular, through measures related to bank accounts, commercial interests, stocks and properties in foreign countries, and applications for residence status and visas.

Indeed, the broader challenge is to develop effective sanctions which wholly avoid punishing civilians. One example is to place sanctions on transit rights, along with selective air and sea boycotts (except for transport of essential humanitarian goods). Other examples might be to pose limits on representation in inter-government forums; or cancel military cooperation agreements, including training and representation abroad. Yet another involves the refusal to provide arms to sanctioned regimes — including the shipment of arms already sold or promised. To date, the practical effect of arms embargoes has simply been to raise the price of arms. We must move towards commitment on the part of arms-producing countries to improve significantly the monitoring of arms transfers — in effect, to police their own dealings rigorously.

■ *Include a provision for humanitarian exceptions in any sanctions regime*, together with the means to make it effective. No exception will work if there are no national or international resources to draw upon. The processing of requests under the exception should be much more expeditious and contain some elements of automaticity for UN agencies, the ICRC, and reputable humanitarian NGOs. A review and evaluation of the work of the Council's sanctions committees in relation to the impacts on civilians should be undertaken. In general, methods and procedures should be expedited.

■ *Undertake a regular evaluation by the Council of the potential and actual humanitarian effects of sanctions on the country.* Rigorous criteria must be developed for judging their impact, particularly on the most marginalised and vulnerable members of society. The UN Secretary-General should also make available the following mechanisms:

a. Prior to imposing sanctions, an appraisal of their potential effects on ordinary people, and suggested measures to avoid them.
b. After the entry into force of the sanctions regime, a regular evaluation of its impact on civilians and the changes necessary to counter negative impacts.
c. To carry out such assessments and/or evaluations, the assistance of concerned international and financial institutions, relevant inter-government and regional organisations, and NGOs, should be sought.

To this end, appropriate systems must be developed for regular, unimpeded monitoring, evaluation, and dissemination of data concerning the social and economic impact of sanctions.

When a crisis affecting the ordinary population is about to arise within a targeted country, it is essential that such situations be brought immediately to the attention of the Security Council, and that specific corrective steps be outlined; uniformity of assessment criteria and of sanctions rulings is vital.

■ In conflict-ridden societies, humanitarian activities are often under way before sanctions were applied. The right of the general population to bodily integrity and subsistence goods should not be violated. Thus, *the authorities of the targeted country and of the different factions and parties to the conflict must commit themselves to ensuring a continuous, impartial, and expeditious delivery of humanitarian assistance.* This includes the following:

a. Access to the necessary information required by UN and non-government humanitarian agencies.
b. No action to obstruct the day-to-day activities of relief workers.
c. Guarantees of the security of humanitarian personnel, their offices, homes, and operational sites.
d. Unimpeded access to conflict areas, and the use of ports, airfields, roads and other infrastructure.

The sanctions regime should consider strict measures to ensure compliance with the above.

■ More generally, *sanctions regimes should have clear objectives for regular review, and precise conditions for being lifted.* These could entail clear warnings that sanctions are likely to be applied as a consequence of specific actions; specifying an agreed time-frame for evaluating the extension, modification, or lifting of the sanctions; and outlining provisions for progressive, partial, or early lifting (including the precise steps required from the target country).

Conclusions

Even with strengthened protections on paper for humanitarian workers, and even with the involvement of humanitarian agencies in measures to ensure that sanctions do not become 'the enemy of the good', the Security Council is ultimately a tool of governments. It can play a strong humanitarian role only at their behest.

Without the political will truly to avoid conflict, or to make the hard sacrifices necessary to preserve peace and promote long-lasting security, there is little guarantee that humanitarianism will not become deeply mired in its own inherent contradictions. For much humanitarian 'relief' today appears even to its most ardent supporters to be a sticking plaster over the scars of years of social and economic decay, which have festered to the point that open wounds confront us with the raw reality of women, children, and the elderly alike becoming the targets of snipers — along with the people seeking to assist them.

What can we do to stem the tide of brutality and impunity? How can we heal the wounds of conflict that tear apart even societies which appear to be 'at peace'? Taking note and calling upon our governments to make human concerns central to statecraft is the first and most important step. Only when we are truly able to ensure the security of people will the Security Council itself have succeeded in its mission.

Well beyond the Council's immediate reach are the societies of its member States—indeed, all members of the family of nations. The challenge is to find ways to enthuse civil society with a renewed understanding of the contemporary means to pursue peace and security—beyond the sometimes cynical and narrowly political aims of 'diplomacy' as traditionally practised.

Among the most committed people working to achieve these aims are, in fact, individuals such as Jimmy Carter, Julius Nyerere, and Oscar Arias — all of whom have actively participated in politics at the highest level, none of whom has lost sight of the humanism which must be at the heart of humanitarianism.

If I end by mentioning outstanding personalities, it is because there is no substitute for the commitment of individual human beings within government and civil society who *want to make a difference*, who are prepared to act on the basis of values and vision that are rooted in the belief that human beings can ultimately find solutions to seemingly insoluble problems.

Cynics would have us believe that there is no space for values in the globalised world of today — cynics who, in the words of Oscar Wilde, 'know the price of everything and the value of nothing'. Yet we know from historical experience that humanitarian agencies in the past have always had to swim against the current, in a never-ending struggle to promote and protect the dignity of people. We know that we will not give in to the moral indifference of our days and that our ethical convictions and political decision to act are far from being exhausted. We are many and enough with the passion to make our world a better place to live.

Notes

1 An edited version of the Gilbert Murray Memorial Lecture delivered at the Sheldonian Theatre in Oxford on 26 June 1996. Professor Gilbert Murray was a founder of the Oxford Committee for Famine Relief (Oxfam) in 1942.

2 *The International Response to Conflict and Genocide: Lessons from the Rwanda Experience — Synthesis Report*, vol. 5 in a series commissioned by the Steering Committee of the Joint Evaluation of Emergency Assistance to Rwanda; ISBN: 87-7265-335-3. This report was prepared collectively by, among others, 19 OECD multilateral donor agencies, nine multilateral and UN agencies, representatives of the International Red Cross and Red Crescent Movement, representatives of major NGO networks worldwide, and expert advisers from regional diplomatic and policy circles. Among the many policy recommendations advanced in the report, I would emphasise the idea that

the Security Council '[should] establish a specialised humanitarian sub-committee [whose purpose] would be to inform fully the Council of developments and concerns regarding humanitarian dimensions of complex emergencies linked to conflict, and to make appropriate recommendations' thereupon. It could be set up as a Joint Committee with ECOSOC under Article 65.

3 See S/PRST/1996/4 of 24 January 1996.

4 See S/PRST/1996/16 of 9 April 1996.

5 See the report of the Informal Open-ended Working Group of the General Assembly on an Agenda for Peace, Sub-group on the Question of United Nations-imposed Sanctions, dated 10 July 1996.

6 Sister Mary Evelyn Jegen, 'Towards a Framework for International Sanctions Policy', Memorandum prepared 18 April 1996.

7 Unpublished working paper by David Cortright, submitted in May 1996; see also D. Cortright and G. Lopez (eds.), *Economic Sanctions: Panacea or Peacebuilding in a Post-Cold War World?*, Boulder, CO: Westview Press (1995).

8 See SC/RES/687 of 3 April 1991.

9 Many of the suggestions below are mentioned in a 'non-paper' on the humanitarian impact of sanctions, circulated among the members of the Security Council (S/1995/300) in April 1996, and in corresponding individual country responses. See also a Report of the Inter-Agency Standing Committee (XIV meeting, 19 April 1996), prepared in conjunction with the DHA (Geneva).

10 Ibid, see footnote 2.

■ **Ambassador Juan Somavía** *is the Permanent Representative of Chile to the United Nations, and served in this capacity on the UN Security Council during 1996–97. He was Chair of the 1995 World Summit for Social Development, and is Chairman of the Board of the UN Research Institute for Social Development (UNRISD). He is currently (1998) Director General elect of the International Labour Organization (ILO).*

This paper was first published in Development in Practice *Volume 7, Number 4, in 1997.*

African rural labour and the World Bank: an alternative perspective

Deborah Fahy Bryceson and John Howe

Globalisation, the academically fashionable theme of the 1990s, has been adapted to the promotional needs of the World Bank in its *World Development Report 1995*, entitled *Workers in an Integrating World*. Appealing to a wide non-technical audience, this report focuses on labour trends in the global marketplace. Despite the weight of the World Bank's influence on economic policy in Sub-Saharan Africa, the report has been economical in its review of past and future trends on the continent. There is, however, one graph which starkly depicts the World Bank's projections for rural Africa. A log-scale histogram (reproduced here as Figure 1) compares incomes of categories of workers in 1992 with their projected income in the year 2010 under 'convergent' and 'divergent' scenarios. In both the baseline and the projected years, African farmers are at the bottom of the histogram, while OECD skilled workers are at the top. The distance between the two groups in 1992 is a factor of about 60:1 (p.119). Projections for the year 2010 show this gap widening in the divergent scenario to 70:1 and narrowing to 50:1 in the convergent scenario.[1] The caption reads: *'All workers stand to benefit from good policy; but the international wage hierarchy will not flatten rapidly.'*

From an Africanist perspective, this graph cannot pass without comment. It implies that the structural-adjustment policies of the past 15 years, in combination with future policy measures along recommended lines, will in fact have little positive impact on African rural producers. This article considers why this may be so, juxtaposing some of the underlying causes of African farmers' poor prospects with the viability of the World Bank's recommendations.

The first section reviews the general approach and depiction of the dynamics of the world economy of the *World Development Report 1995*

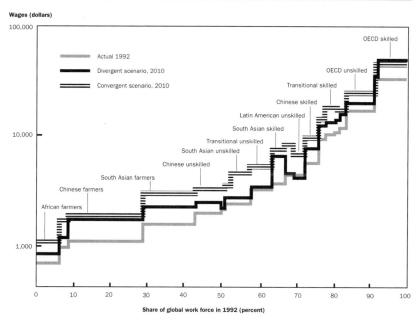

Figure 1
Actual and projected wages and employment shares by region and skill level

Wages (dollars)

Legend:
- Actual 1992
- Divergent scenario, 2010
- Convergent scenario, 2010

Labels (left to right): African farmers, Chinese farmers, South Asian farmers, Chinese unskilled, South Asian unskilled, Transitional unskilled, South Asian skilled, Latin American unskilled, Chinese skilled, Transitional skilled, OECD unskilled, OECD skilled

Share of global work force in 1992 (percent)

Wages are in 1992 international prices, scaled logarithmically. Each group's share of the global work force is indicated by the length of its horizontal line segment. Unlabelled line segments represent groups accounting individually for less than 2.5 per cent of the global workforce (10 per cent in total). The scenarios as depicted use 1992 workforce shares, not those projected for 2010. 'Transitional' refers to the former centrally planned economies of Europe and Central Asia.

Source: World Bank 1995, based on Lewis, Robinson, and Wang, background paper; World Bank staff estimates.

(*WDR95*). Using evidence from Ghana and Tanzania, two countries which are often cited as examples of the successful application of structural adjustment, we go on to consider recent African agricultural performance. In a broad review of literature, documented social and political tendencies are related to Sub-Saharan Africa's (SSA) current economic policies and performance. The imbalances of rural labour displacement are highlighted, and measures to address the growing problem are sketched before the conclusion.

World Bank prescriptions for labour in the global market

The core argument of *WDR95* is that 'workers of the world' are being increasingly incorporated into open, international markets characterised by the accelerated flow of information, goods, and capital. In absolute numbers, the global labour force has grown massively in the last three decades, from roughly 1.25 billion people of working age in 1965 to twice as many in 1995. It is expected to triple in the next thirty years (p.7). Demographically, by far the greatest increases in the future labour force will be observed in the poorer regions of the world.

In the light of these trends, two phenomena are highlighted. While the size of the work force has doubled, average work productivity has also doubled. This leads to the conclusion that 'the world's median worker is better off today than 30 years ago' (p.9). However, productivity gains have been unequally distributed, causing the increased prosperity of the last thirty years to be unevenly distributed. Divergence, not convergence, between rich and poor workers in the world is the result. In fact, this diverging trend has entrenched itself over the last century. In 1870, the average per capita income in the rich countries was 11 times higher than that of the poorest. In 1960 the ratio rose to 38 and by 1985 it was 52 (p.9). Despite these daunting statistics, the report reaches the conclusion that inequality between the rich and the poor need not grow further. A new phase of convergence can be achieved with the 'right domestic and international policies' (p.8).

In order to illustrate the meaning and rewards of the 'right policies', the report classifies development strategies geographically. Policies in East Asian countries are characterised as outward-looking and market-oriented, whereas countries in Sub-Saharan Africa, Latin America, and the Middle East form a second category which largely pursued 'inward-oriented development paths, protecting certain industries and over-taxing their agricultural sectors' (p.13). Finally the former centrally planned economies of Eastern Europe and Central Asia are described as those where market mechanisms were removed in favour of State control. Predictably, the report pronounces the latter two as 'inevitable dead ends' (p.14) and praises East Asian examples, notably those of Korea, Indonesia, Malaysia, and China.

The *WDR95* raises the question of whether globalisation, characterised by large increases in international trade, greater flows of international capital, and increased human migration pose a threat or alternatively offer opportunities to workers. It is argued that workers have generally been helped by the expansion of world trade in labour-intensive manufactured goods and larger flows of private capital directed to developing countries. Statistics are cited to show that, in countries with higher than average growth in exports, real wages grew faster than in those where exports were relatively stagnant. The international market is seen as a vista of opportunity, freeing workers and capital holders from the constraints imposed by small domestic markets.

A second manifestation of globalisation is the increasing volume and mobility of capital flows. In its worldwide search for high returns, private capital — i.e. foreign direct investment — has flowed to low-income and middle-income countries at record levels in recent years. The *WDR95* admits that dangers and risks may arise as the ability of governments to tax capital is limited. Excessively flexible capital may move in when wages are low and depart when they rise. 'Footloose investments' (p.62) may generate instability in poor countries. None the less, the advantages of attracting more external capital are stressed. It is anticipated that higher capital-intensity of labour will boost workers' productivity, permit wage increases, and enable developing countries to take advantage of new trade opportunities.

Increased international migration, the third phenomenon associated with globalisation, is more politically charged. Here the report denies the virtues of free movement. While recognising the gains which international migration may bring in the form of remittances and lower production costs for sending and receiving countries respectively, the report warns that completely free labour mobility could induce large-scale immigration to rich countries, 'producing equally large social dislocations there' (p.67). Thus, migratory flows must be managed to minimise cultural resistance and economic costs to unskilled native workers (p. 68).

Overall, the combination of greater integration in a global market and the right development strategy is professed to offer a scenario of 'inclusion and convergence', which could begin to reverse the large and growing welfare gap between the world's rich and poor.

African performance under structural adjustment

In comparison with other regions of the world, African economic performance indicators evince a continental 'drag effect'. Output measurements like GNP, export earnings, and capital endowments such as infrastructure and skills are on average the world's lowest. World Bank reasoning explains this as the legacy of 'bad' policies, such as industrial protectionism and urban bias.

By designating agricultural export as the key to Africa's economic future, international terms of trade for African products take on central importance. Ignoring the critique of the notion of urban bias (for example, Jamal and Weeks 1988; Bryceson 1992), as well as Africa's handicapped historical starting point as a largely agrarian zone of subsistence producers, the World Bank proceeds to undermine the logic of its own argument by relegating the international terms of trade that African agrarian producers now face to the position of an external factor. When declining terms of trade are mentioned in the text, they are seen more as a contextual problem, with a consequent diminution of their value in explaining African export performance. Can the global market offer opportunities to African smallholders while prices continue to fall for major export crops? The economic performance of Tanzania and Ghana is illustrative of trends in East and West Africa.

The example of Tanzania

In Tanzania, coffee earnings dropped from US$185 million in 1986 to US$77 million in 1991, as a result of the dramatic decline in world-market coffee prices. In 1992, coffee farmers were paid 97 per cent of world-market prices, up from 38 per cent in 1989. None the less, they received almost identical nominal producer prices in both years. In the words of Putterman (1995:321): 'the Tanzanian producer is in no more profitable position after than before liberalisation'. There were signs of a growing diversification of the economic base of households, but this came largely through petty-income earnings, not throught the revival of traditional exports such as coffee, cotton, and cashews, induced by structural adjustment programmes (SAPs). Similarly, Bagachwa et al. (1995) point to the burgeoning informal 'second economy'.

Food-crop production has been variable. Tanzania was fortunate in implementing its first phase of market liberalisation during years of favourable rainfall, such that supplies of the main marketed staples were plentiful (Bryceson 1993). However, by the mid-1990s, the spiralling cost of food-crop inputs and declining real producer-prices of food crops in areas away from the main transport corridors had drastically reduced incentives to farmers. This was especially true in the formerly important 'Big Four' regions, Mbeya, Rukwa, Ruvuma, and Iringa, which had served as the nation's granary under pre-SAPs pan-territorial pricing policies.

The example of Ghana

In Ghana, structural adjustment put great emphasis on the revitalisation of the cocoa sector and drastic increases in producer prices which, when combined with improved rainfall conditions after 1983, raised output from 154,000 tons in 1983 to 228,000 in 1988 (Sarris and Shams 1991). However, export values fell thereafter, with the result that in 1991, after debt servicing, Ghana's export receipts covered only 56 per cent of the value of its imports (Parfitt 1995:62). Moreover, the gains following the expansion of cocoa output were rewards to a relatively small sector of the cocoa farms. One third of the cocoa farmers, namely the larger-scale farmers, received 94 per cent of total gross income from cocoa (Kraus 1991:26). Pearce (1992:41) questions the strategy of relying on export-led growth, 'because any increase in Ghana's cocoa production may serve more to drive down world prices than to raise foreign exchange earnings'. Sarris and Shams (1991) point to evidence that structural adjustment undermined Ghanaian agriculture by raising the costs of agricultural inputs and causing a drastic decline in the share of government expenditure going to the agricultural sector. The drop in the budgetary allocation from 10.4 per cent in 1983 to 3.5 per cent in 1989 resulted in insufficient funding for the effective functioning of the Ministry of Agriculture.

Until 1983, producer prices for food had increased faster than cocoa prices. Thereafter, the trend was reversed. By turning the domestic terms of trade dramatically against food producers, the goal of food self-sufficiency was hindered (Kusi 1991). Food production still provides the main source of income to most Ghanaian smallholders; and returns from maize, rice, and cassava sharply declined in the latter half of the 1980s. The strong emphasis placed by SAP on cost-recovery and privatisation has increased smallholders' need for cash and led to greater indebtedness in informal credit systems, where interest rates are high. According to some observers, this has aggravated socio-economic differentiation and the marginalisation of smallholders (Kusi 1991, Sarris and Shams 1991).

In both Tanzania and Ghana, growing unemployment, resulting in tens of thousands of public and private workers being laid off, could be interpreted as a waste of resources. It is not uncommon to find university-educated people involved in farming and petty trade activities which in no way match their educational qualifications. A 1989 US congressional mission to Ghana did not hesitate to criticise these 'harsh and ill planned policies' of trimming public-sector employment. Furthermore, the SAPs austerity measures have led to severe cuts in health and education expenditure, representing setbacks to human-capital formation.

Ironically, the World Bank's review of progress under structural adjustment stated that 'Ghana can profit from East Asia's experience by emphasising ... education and health' (World Bank 1994:40).

In their comparison of patterns of development world-wide, Syrquin and Chenery (1989) argue that the rise in the ratio of human (and physical) capital to labour is a characteristic feature of the development trajectory. But the reverse is true for Africa. Under SAPs, the continent is in danger of becoming entrapped in a vicious cycle of disinvestment in human capital, resulting in lower productivity and leading to disincentives to future investment, which further reduce human-capital levels relative to the rest of the world.

A comparative advantage for African agriculture?

Underpinning the *WDR95*'s comparison of regional economic performance in the global market is a model of transition from low-productivity, labour-intensive agriculture to high-productivity, capital-intensive services and industry. Sub-Saharan Africa, representative of the lower end of the transitional spectrum, is naturally assumed to have a comparative advantage in agriculture. Is there any basis for assuming that Sub-Saharan Africa can compete in the world market on the basis of its under-capitalised peasant agriculture?

SSA's competitiveness in foreign markets throughout this century has been handicapped by high transport costs. The vast distances of the continent, combined with the exceptionally poor transport infrastructure of rail and road, put African exports at a gross disadvantage relative to the tropical products of Latin America and South East Asia. The transport constraint extends right down to the peasant household. Most agricultural field-to-home transport is based on female porterage.

Africa's competitiveness is conditioned by the limited range of its agricultural exports. The beverage crops — coffee, cocoa, and tea — account for 52 per cent of total agricultural export earnings (UNCTAD 1987, 1991). These crops, in particular coffee and cocoa, have been hit especially hard by deteriorating international prices. The rise in coffee prices in 1993-94, due to the failure of the Brazilian harvest, provided a considerable boost to many African coffee-exporting countries; but market analysts see this as a temporary blip on the otherwise entrenched downward price path.

Yields and the quality of many peasant-produced African exports have suffered under structural adjustment. Government agricultural extension services, input subsidies, and quality controls have been drastically reduced, and the private sector has not provided adequate substitutes. Coffee is again illustrative. The declining quality of export products, due to new marketing agents' lack of experience in grading, transporting, and storing valuable export crops since market liberalisation in 1994, has undermined the export standards of Tanzanian *arabica* coffee, once known for its high quality. In 1995, buyers complained about an unusually high moisture content and the mixing of grades of coffee. Only a quarter of the 50,000 tonnes produced was of exportable quality.

Hostile international market conditions for African products are embedded not only in the long-term decline in prices for major export crops, but also in the terms of the recently concluded Uruguay Round of trade negotiations, culminating in the establishment of the World Trade Organisation. As a result of the agreement, Sub-Saharan African trade preferences in European Union markets will be eroded, with the possibility of further loss of market shares. Furthermore, the prices of tropical export crops are expected to drop relative to grain — which penalises most African countries, which are net importers of grain.

It is debatable if the small-scale family production of peasant agriculture has a promising future anywhere in the world. The tendency in global agricultural development is for increasing capitalisation, which implies large-scale and often industrial-type production. Supermarket conglomerates, whose inordinate influence on demand specifications (such as the timing and scale of delivery, in addition to stable prices) is transforming agricultural markets, are now increasingly characterised by scheduled delivery of large consignments, minimising the effect of seasonal, fluctuating supplies. European and North American agriculture, as well as large-scale plantations in the developing world using scientific advances in agriculture such as bio-technology and hydroponics, can meet the specifications of such markets (Carruthers 1994). African peasant production cannot. It is the antithesis of highly standardised production and strict delivery schedules.

Not only do tendencies towards more highly capitalised agriculture worldwide reduce the market for African smallholders' existing production. They also severely undermine African farmers' attempts (endorsed by the World Bank) to diversify agricultural exports. Horticultural products are a prime example. They are suggested as non-traditional export crops which Africa should endeavour to produce. But horticultural markets already face conditions of over-supply. In the Netherlands, it is predicted that smaller-scale farmers will be edged out of the market by larger producers. If highly capitalised Dutch farmers, ever attuned to markets, cannot compete, the prospects of African smallholders trying to break into the market are very slim indeed. African smallholder farmers have very little room for manoeuvre in international agricultural markets both now and for the foreseeable future, despite the World Bank's endorsement of them as efficient producers (p.26).

Karl Polanyi (1957) drew attention to the labour-dislocating impact of global markets in his historical review of the effects of American and Australian grain imports on nineteenth-century European peasant farming:

> International free trade, if unchecked, must necessarily eliminate ever-larger compact bodies of agricultural producers. This inevitable process of destruction was very much aggravated by ... the great investments involved in the building of steamships and railroads ... whole continents were opened up and an avalanche of grain descended upon unhappy Europe ... Central Europe, facing utter destruction of its rural society, was forced to protect its peasantry by introducing corn laws. (Polanyi 1957)

Given the current climate of market liberalism and the power of international financial institutions over policies in developing countries, protectionist measures are ruled out as an option for the peasantries of today. 'Labour flight' is a more likely prospect. Urban migration to national and regional capitals has reached very high levels in several countries. City streets are swamped with petty traders.[2] For the more adventurous, international migration to Europe or the United States is the goal.[3] There is irony in this, given that 'labour flight' is the one feature of globalisation that the World Bank does not sanction.

Agricultural prospects as perceived by African farmers

The actions and attitudes of African producers themselves cannot be ignored. In a wide array of field studies across the continent, a process of 'de-agrarianisation', involving the reorientation of economic activity away from farming within rural areas or alternatively residential relocation in urban settings, has been documented (Bryceson 1995). These occupational and locational shifts often have distinct demographic patterns. A strong generational divide is emerging in many areas. Youth are flocking into petty trading activities. The low and uncertain returns from smallholder production lead even uneducated youth without urban job prospects to seek alternatives to farming.

While much has been written about the effects of economic liberalisation on African production, little attention has been paid to its impact on consumption. For most of the African population, especially young people, it is the availability of a wider array of consumer goods which has been the most significant aspect of liberalisation. Many African countries have been awash with cheap imports of Asian consumer goods, which have displaced the more erratic supplies of African manufacturers. The importation of clothing and beauty products, as well as more expensive music, TV, and video equipment, has led African youth to assimilate many of the features of Western mass consumption. Their heightened economic independence, arising from the diversification of household livelihood, as each member seeks income-earning activities, has laid the foundation for what might be best termed youth sub-cultures, not unlike those found in industrialised countries. But the purchase of such consumer goods requires cash earnings, which are not easily derived from agricultural production subject to declining world-market prices. Thus cash incomes are sought in the sphere of petty trade, while more lucrative earnings can be derived from the contraband trade in ivory, gold, diamonds or drugs (Ellis and MacGaffey, 1996).

Several countries have witnessed a rise in contraband trade and not infrequently attendant violence and crime (Nkera and Schoepf 1991). In the extreme, there is the diamond trade of Liberia and Sierra Leone, so lucrative that many political commentators argue that the civil wars in these countries orbit around its control (Richards 1995). Other more peaceful countries have also experienced rising crime associated with contraband goods, especially drugs. For example, authorities are increasingly concerned with the volume of drugs trafficked through Tanzania, whereas 15 years ago drug trading was negligible. Nigeria and, to a growing extent, South Africa have emerged as African entrepôts for the international drug trade.

Economic liberalisation has been accompanied by cultural scepticism on the part of young people: now well aware of alternative lifestyles through the West-dominated media, they are dissatisfied with agrarian values and livelihoods (Savishinsky 1994, Beckerleg 1995). They are experimenting with alternative production and consumption patterns in their search for a better material life. This search can be creative and beneficial or detrimental and politically destabilising, with an increasing incidence of crime, violence, and civil disorder.

Economic and political trends tend to reinforce each other. The economic implosion caused by stabilisation measures has dashed the expectations of many segments of the urban and rural population, who, after more than two decades of declining standards of living, were hoping for some material gain. Multi-party elections are also producing mixed results. In some cases, such as the 1994 election in Malawi, they have succeeded in undermining despotic regimes. In others, they have met with rural apathy and political campaigns devoid of issues, in which candidates must whip up support by emphasising religious or ethnic divisions; an example of this is the recent emergence of Christian/Islamic divisions in the 1995 Tanzanian election. At worst, as in the Burundian election of 1993, this process acted as a catalyst in the fomentation of civil war.

In the World Bank's linear model of economic growth, the possibility that countries at the lower end of the spectrum might experience retrogression, dropping into circumstances of minus growth, is not entertained. Yet with the increasing incidence of civil disturbances, war, and refugee flight in SSA, it would be useful to analyse the minus-growth scenario, particularly because such circumstances prompt expensive humanitarian interventions.[4]

Confronting rural labour displacement and its social consequences

Political matters are beyond the purview of the WDR95, which presents a more ordered world in which nation-states, supported by peasant economies, ascend from labour-intensive agriculture to capital-intensive industry, and in so doing switch from an informal to a formal economy and higher levels of productivity. The mechanisms whereby increasing use of technology and its obvious labour-displacing outcomes can ensure increasing formal employment and income for populations are not explained. The fact that the economies of most industrial countries have failed to generate jobs, and unemployment rates have steadily edged upwards since World War II, makes it unlikely that developing countries, especially those starting at the technological levels now prevailing in SSA, can generate sufficient jobs for agricultural producers involved in voluntary or involuntary redundancy.

The report neglects the possibility of international market competition leading to redundancy for smallholder farmers in Africa or elsewhere in the developing world. Rather, it tries to allay fears regarding the redundancy of unskilled and semi-skilled workers in advanced industrialised countries who are predicted to be out-competed by lower-income wage workers in developing countries, particularly in Asia (p.58).

Since the problem of rural labour displacement is not acknowledged, its solution is never mooted. The African countryside must make do with the *WDR95*'s promise of 'global convergence'.

Less than one per cent of the world's direct private investment goes to Africa. Significant foreign investment on any meaningful scale has been restricted to oil-rich Nigeria and a few other mineral-exporting countries (Kraus 1992). Even if investment in mining and capitalised agriculture assumed significant dimensions, it is improbable, given the capital-bias of Western investment patterns, that job creation would begin to match the rate of agricultural labour displacement. It is in this context that the problem of rural labour displacement should be situated and measures taken to address it. Many if not most countries in Africa would benefit from 'special programmes' of a national dimension.

The benefits of public-works schemes

Employment-creating programmes which draw on SSA's growing supply of under-employed rural labour are a means of addressing peasant labour displacement before it reaches crisis proportions. Labour-intensive public works can provide physical infrastructure such as roads, water supplies, housing, electricity, and improved communications, all of which can expand or renew the physical infrastructure of rural Africa.

Through several large-scale programmes and pilot projects in a number of African countries, it has been demonstrated that labour-intensive methods of construction have several advantages over the usual capital-intensive methods (Ghana: Bentall 1993; Kenya: de Veen 1983; Malawi: Hagen and Relf 1988; Lesotho: Marshall 1990; Botswana: Brudefors 1991; continental: Howe and Bantje 1995).

- Firstly, if properly planned and managed, they offer lower production costs, while maintaining technical quality standards.
- Secondly, there are substantial savings in foreign-exchange costs. Labour-intensive methods significantly reduce the need for importation of heavy capital machinery and are not prone to the same delays in production schedules and the expenses incurred by poorly maintained and/or malfunctioning equipment.
- Thirdly, they can offer mass employment of a short- to medium-term nature.
- Fourthly, labour-intensive earthworks have been shown to be less harmful to the natural environment (Howe and Mueller 1995).
- Fifthly, labour-creating public works can be designed to suit the

livelihood needs of the most needy in the rural community. This has been shown to be the case especially for land-poor female heads of households (Bryceson and Howe 1993).

- Finally, in line with current emphasis on the role of the market, labour-intensive methods can be adopted by small private contractors more easily than capital-intensive techniques, which require heavy investment in machinery (Henley 1984, Musumba 1993).

There are potential educational and occupational benefits which await the implementation of labour-creating public works on a larger regional or national scale. At present, school enrolment is low in most countries in Africa. Labour-intensive public works, if implemented with care, could serve as post-formal education for raising non-agrarian as well as agrarian skills and productivity (Bryceson and Howe 1995). In so doing, there would be the possibility of creating new occupational and professional identities, particularly for the benefit of young people, who may then grasp the opportunities that have eluded their parents' generation. Most importantly, labour-creating public works constitute human-capital investment which not only enhances the life-long earning capacity of the individual involved, but lends more versatility at an aggregate level to the national economy.

In the face of these realised and potential benefits, it is necessary to ask why labour-creating methods have not been taken more seriously to date. Firstly, over the last 20 years, labour-intensive public works have been over-identified with hastily executed *relief* works, which have had as their main and often only objective the immediate survival of distressed people in emergency situations. Relief operations have to be executed quickly to address people's acute needs for food, shelter, or income. They often have a 'make work' or 'disguised dole' image which is inimical to acceptance of their use for properly engineered products. Politicians want quick results and are impatient with those defending the virtues of a careful and necessarily slow process of establishment (Howe and Bantje 1995). Concern for the quality or durability of any infrastructural works that result from the investments are necessarily second-order considerations. By contrast, the development of useful and sustainable infrastructure is an inherently slow process of planning, design, training, implementation, and maintenance, with different gestation periods, organisational requirements, and criteria of success. Critics have failed to recognise that labour-intensive public works for relief and development are distinct and counter-opposed. Labour-based relief works have an immediacy and political imperative which militate against the success of development-oriented labour-creating public works aimed at training, infrastructure building, and employment generation. The order of these objectives is deliberate: the rate at which labour-intensive public works should expand is dictated by the rate at which the specially trained technicians, supervisors, and managers can be produced.

Secondly, commercial biases of the international engineering profession provide a strong counterforce to the adoption of labour-intensive methods of construction. Labour-creating public works restrict the need for importation of expensive capital equipment and expertise — a strategy which is in direct conflict with international corporate interests and the technical orientation of engineers trained in Western industrialised countries.

Thirdly, structural adjustment policies promoting market liberalisation and cutbacks in State expenditure have cast a shadow on the role of the State in development initiatives. There is a common misconception that public works must necessarily be exclusively 'public', i.e. State-funded and State-executed. This masks the fact that the private sector can play an active role in construction activities from the outset and may eventually eliminate the need for State funding. There are various possible permutations of partnership between the State and the private sector. However, at the outset, the State would logically have a central role in initiating large-scale infrastructure-provisioning public-works programmes. The State's initiating and possibly coordinating role raises the question of finance and donor support.

In this era of donor fatigue, many bi-lateral donors are warning that African countries must be weaned from dependence on foreign aid. A gradual disengagement is advocated, eased by generous debt-relief. Nonetheless, cognisant of the precarious economic position of most African countries *vis à vis* the world market, the United Nations has recognised the value of a concerted injection of capital into flagging African economies. In March 1996, the UN-sponsored African System-wide Special Initiative on Africa was announced, with the aim of disbursing US$25 billion over a ten-year period, concentrating on investment in water supply, food security, governance, social and human development, and resource mobilisation. Will this investment be labour-intensive or capital-intensive in nature? In other words, will it exacerbate or alleviate rural labour displacement?

Labour-creating public-work programmes have been implemented with notable success in several places in rural Africa, but there is a need to scale-up and revise such programmes to address the continental problem of rural labour displacement. Despite general calls for human-capital investment in Africa, the *WDR95* perceives public works primarily in terms of their role in provisioning infrastructure in situations of disaster or poverty relief (p.47). A much longer-term perspective on human-capital investment is required, in view of the continent's declining capacity for provisioning public education and the paucity of private foreign capital flowing to Africa. Labour-creating public works of a high engineering and organisational standard offer several proven and potential benefits. The design of programmes would have to suit specific national needs, as well as regional labour-market characteristics, and, in their initial stages, most would require donor finance and possibly some expertise. Such infrastructure and employment opportunities would constitute a vital part of the necessary material basis for non-agrarian activities in rural economies with lasting labour-absorption capacity.

Conclusions: African farmers' short-straw draw

The *WDR95* combines two main themes: labour and the global market. In the context of economic and technological change in the late twentieth century, this is a document celebrating the 'triumph of the market', seen as an overall gain for the world. Such a stance is possible, given the notion that every society is fundamentally amenable to the 'will' of the market. Rather than seeing policies as a result of a balance of various political and social forces, the World Bank's market philosophy is imbued with fundamentalist notions of inherent 'good' and 'bad'. The ideological fervour of the text does not permit a sober consideration of current trends in international capital investment and the increasing aggregation of production in the agricultural sector world-wide. Rather, the reader is obliged to believe that there is a free play of demand and supply, and that the unfettered mobility of capital is an unquestionable good, whereas the mobility of labour must be kept in check for 'cultural coherence'. The inexorable growth of wealth disparities under capital is seen as an aberration. Adam Smith's 'hidden hand' is assumed to have the power to smooth things out for the eventual benefit of all.

The overall message of *WDR95* to the African smallholder is that those who engage in production for the global market are all potential winners in the lottery. What is not stressed is that the losers are not randomly selected. Invariably those producers with lower endowments of capital and market information constitute the fallout. African smallholders, the world's most technologically handicapped and marginalised agrarian producers, are doomed to fail. The truth lies in the graph (p.121), not in the text about policy reform for Africa.

Through the dissemination of information via the Western-dominated media, as well as through the conspicuous enrichment of certain urban-based and/or capitalist investors within Africa, peasant farmers are becoming well aware of what they do not have. 'Enterprising' Africans, especially young ones, are finding unconventional short-cuts out of the quagmire, some of which are politically and socially destabilising, as witnessed in a number of countries already. In the absence of economic measures to address the deficit in skills, and the yawning gap between the expectations of the rural populace and actual returns to their labour, the *WDR95*'s optimism, reflected in the title *Workers in an Integrating World,* is misplaced as far as Africa is concerned. *Farmers in a Disintegrating Continent* would be a more appropriate description of the forces at work.

Investment in human capital, alongside efforts to encourage smallholder agricultural growth, is a frontal way of arresting Africa's downward slide in the global market. Because returns on labour-intensive public works and vocational-training investment are initially low, the market itself is unlikely to initiate such movement. The first and possibly the interim steps must be made by the major stakeholders in African peace and prosperity, namely African governments and the international community, providing the jump-start needed for the effective operation of market forces in African nation-states.

Acknowledgement

We are indebted to Marius de Langen, Patricia Paravano, and Yohannes Habtu for their comments and to Henk Meilink for in-depth discussion about the content of this paper. None of them, however, bears responsibility for the views expressed.

Notes

1 Factors are estimated from the graphical representation, since absolute values are not given.

2 For example, according to the Chair of the Dar es Salaam City Commission, the city had 650,000 hawkers from up-country regions, a situation which 'would be unmanageable if further influx was not curbed' ('City Commission Opts for Dialogue with Petty Traders', *Daily News* 23/8/96). The Chairman of the Law Reform Commission voiced concern that 'If Tanzania chooses to neglect the growing number of unemployed youths in towns and the rural side, it will face unprecedented problems in the next 20 years' ('Legislators and Lawyers Plead for Retention of "Nguvu Kazi" Act', *Guardian* (DSM), 13/4/96).

3 Perhaps appreciative of the pressures of labour dislocation in Africa, the European Union has embarked on the construction of a 8.5 km wall, valued at US$29 million, to be built to surround Ceuta, a Spanish enclave on the north African coast, to keep illegal immigrants out of Europe ('Europe rebuilds the Wall in Africa', *The European*, 30/11-6/12/95).

4 For example, the price of peace-keeping in a two-year period in Rwanda from April 1994 to March 1996 was US$2.5 billion, a figure which excludes the value of Rwandan lives lost in the conflict ('International Response to Conflict and Genocide: Lessons from the Rwanda Experience', as reported in *Eastern African News*, 12/3/96).

References

Bagachwa, M. S. D. and A. Naho (1995) 'Estimating the second economy in Tanzania', *World Development 23* (8): 1387–99.

Beckerleg, S. (1995) '"Brown sugar" or Friday prayers: youth choices and community building in coastal Kenya', *African Affairs 94* (374): 23–38.

Bentall, P. H. (1993) *Ghana Feeder Roads Project Labour-Based Rehabil-itation and Maintenance*, CTP 116, Geneva: ILO.

Brudefors, U. (1991) LG-34 *Labour Intensive Road Programme (Botswana)*, CTP 43, Geneva: ILO.

Bryceson, D. F. (1992) 'Urban bias revisited: Tanzanian staple food pricing', in C. Hewitt de Alcantara (ed.) *Real Markets: Social and Political Issues of Food Policy Reform*, London: Frank Cass.

Bryceson, D. F. (1993) *Liberalising Tanzania's Food Trade*, London: James Currey.

Bryceson, D. F. (1995) 'Deagrarian-isation and rural employment in sub-Saharan Africa: a sectoral perspective', *World Development 24* (1): 97–112.

Bryceson, D. F. and J. Howe (1993) *Women and Labour-Based Road Works in Sub-Saharan Africa*, Delft: IHE Working Paper IP-4.

Bryceson, D. F. and J. Howe (1995) 'An agrarian continent in transition', in S. Ellis, *Africa Now: People, Policies and Institutions*, London: James Currey.

Carruthers, I. (1994) '2020 vision: dramatic changes in the world agricul-tural and industrial production systems', International Irrigation Management Institute, *IIMI Review* 8(1): 14–20.

Ellis, S. and J. MacGaffey (1996), 'Research on Sub-Saharan Africa's un-recorded trade', *African Studies Review*.

Hagen, S. and C. Relf (1988) *The District Road Improvement and Maintenance Programmes: Malawi*, Geneva: ILO/WEP.

Henley, J. (1984) *Road Maintenance and the Use of Small-Scale Contractors in the Central African Republic*, CTP 38, Geneva: ILO.

Howe, J. and H. Bantje (1995) *Technology Choice in Civil Engineer-ing Practice: Experience in the Road Sector*, CTP 141, Geneva: ILO.

Howe, J. and H. Mueller (1995) *Labour-Based Road Engineering*, Geneva: ILO.

Jamal, V. and J. Weeks (1988) 'The vanishing rural–urban gap in Sub-Saharan Africa', *International Labour Review 127* (3).

Johannessen, B. *Labour-based Technology: A Review of Current Practice,* CTP 133, Geneva: ILO.

Kraus, J. (1991) 'The struggle over structural adjustment in Ghana', *Africa Today*, 4th Quarter, 19–37.

Kraus, J. (1992) 'Debt, structural adjustment and private investment in Africa', in R. A. Ahene and B. S. Katz (eds): *Privatisation and Investment in Sub-Saharan Africa,* New York: Praeger.

Kusi, N. K. (1991) 'Ghana: can the adjustment reforms be sustained?', *Africa Development 1.*

Marshall, J. (1990) *Kingdom of Lesotho, Ministry of Works: The Labour Construction Unit,* CTP 108, Geneva: ILO.

Musumba, W. E. (1993) *Labour-based Contracting: Uganda's Experience,* in Johannessen (ed.).

Nkera, R. and B. G. Schoepf (1991) 'Unrecorded trade in southeast Shaba and across Zaire's southern borders', in J. MacGaffey et al. (eds) *The Real Economy of Zaire: The Contribution of Smuggling and Other Unofficial Activities to National Wealth,* London: James Currey.

Parfitt, T. W. (1995) 'Adjustment for stabilisation or growth? Ghana and the Gambia', *Review of African Political Economy 63.*

Pearce, R. (1992) 'Ghana', in A. Duncan and J. Howell (eds): *Structural Adjustment and the African Farmer,* London: James Currey.

Polanyi, K. (1957) *The Great Transformation: Economic and Political Origins of Our Times,* Boston: Beacon.

Putterman, L. (1995) 'Economic reform and smallholder agriculture in Tanzania: a discussion of recent market liberalisation, road rehabilitation, and technology dissemination efforts', *World Development 23* (2): 311–26.

Richards, P. (1995) 'Liberia and Sierra Leone', in O. W. Furley (ed.): *Conflict in Africa,* London: I.B. Tauris.

Sarris, A. and H. Shams (1991) Ghana under Structural Adjustment: *The Impact on Agriculture and the Rural Poor,* New York: New York University Press.

Savishinsky, N. J. (1994) 'Rastafari in the promised land: the spread of a Jamaican socioreligious movement among the youth of West Africa', *African Studies Review 37* (3): 19–50.

Syrquin, M. and H. B. Chenery (1989) *Patterns of Development, 1950 to 1983,* World Bank Discussion Paper 41, Washington DC.

UNCTAD (1987 and 1991) *Commodity Yearbook,* Geneva.

de Veen, J. J. (1983) *The Rural Access Roads Programme: Appropriate Technology in Kenya,* Geneva: ILO.

World Bank (1994) *Adjustment in Africa: Reform, Results and the Road Ahead,* New York: Oxford University Press.

World Bank (1995) *World Development Report 1995: Workers in an Integrating World,* New York: Oxford University Press.

■ **Deborah Fahy Bryceson** *is a Research Fellow at the Afrika-Studiecentrum (ASC), Leiden.*

■ **John Howe** *is Professor of Infrastructural Planning at the Institute of Infrastructure, Hydraulics and Environmental Engineering (IHE), Delft.*

This paper was first published in Development in Practice, *Volume 7, Number 1, in 1997.*

Empowerment and survival: humanitarian work in civil conflict

Martha Thompson

Introduction

'Wait,' said the guide. 'Soldiers from the Bracamonte Battalion have crossed the river and might climb this hill.' It was April 1989, and a colleague and I were visiting resettlements in the war zones of Chalatenango, in northern El Salvador. In the early 1980s, the military had sacked the area, slaughtering people and destroying their belongings. Survivors fled. From 1983, the Farabundi Martí Liberation Front (FMLN) controlled it, and in 1987 4,500 refugees returned from Honduras. Gradually, more refugees returned to rural Chalatenango, despite the continued conflict. Salvadoran church-based organisations, with co-funding from the British government, were helping these communities to rebuild their lives.

The communities had assigned a 55-year old man, Don Jesús, as our guide on our four-day visit. Like many subsistence farmers, he used to go to the coast for three months a year as a seasonal labourer. He had worked on many plantations, including that of Alfredo Cristiani, the President-elect. *'They say Cristiani is concerned about the poor. But when we were working on his coffee plantation and demanded higher wages, he called in the National Guard to beat us up.'* A month later, I met with a European diplomat in San Salvador. He had recently dined with Cristiani, which had been a delightful experience. The new President was charming, intelligent, concerned about poverty — very different from the usual image of powerful people on the Salvadoran right.

What the diplomat and I saw was the two faces of power: one reserved for equals, and one for inferiors. One's vision of reality is affected by the particular voices one hears. Humanitarian workers were moved and changed by hearing the voice of the poor in El Salvador.

The fact that marginalised people share their perceptions with us gives us a responsibility to bear witness to their situation. This article describes the reality of doing humanitarian work in a prolonged counter-insurgency war, and reflects on working for an international NGO in such a context. It describes how conflict affects our work, our local counterparts, and ourselves.

Background: the 1980–91 war

El Salvador is characterised by an unjust distribution of wealth and resources, and the absence of a fair legal system. These inequities lay behind the eleven-year war, and remain unresolved. Salvadoran society is like a squat pyramid, with the oligarchy as a tiny apex, then a slightly larger layer of military, and a thin stratum of middle-class people; the main substance of the pyramid is formed by desperately poor people. Every second adult is illiterate, and the average daily wage is less than $1. Seven out of ten people are subsistence farmers, and over 75 per cent of the land is still owned by a tiny fraction of the population (a situation little improved by the post-war land agreement). The country was under military rule from 1932 to 1979, with successive coups, State-sponsored violence, and fraudulent elections keeping civilians out of power.

This situation can be traced back to the Conquest. The Spanish who pushed the Indians off their land and forced them to grow indigo were succeeded by the *criollos*, who took land to grow sugar and raise cattle. By the twentieth century, the coffee barons had concentrated land and wealth in the hands of 14 families, who multiplied into the 250 that comprise today's oligarchy.

Rich Salvadorans were used to treating the country like their back-yard. They could take a peasant's land simply by extending their fence around it. A wealthy man could rape a poor woman without a second thought, lend himself money from the national banks, employ the National Guard to round up labourers for his plantations or to kill union workers, and exempt himself from all but minimal taxes, while taxing the poor into starvation. The rich made laws to structure the economy around their needs, and have troublemakers jailed. They controlled everything, using the State to concentrate their power, and the security forces to maintain it.

Their justification was that the poor were less than human and so had no rights. Poor people's land could be taken, but they had no legal redress, and no voice in law-making. Health-care and education were priced out of their grasp, for if they were educated they would cause trouble. They were forcibly recruited into the army, and taxed even for felling a tree on their own land. Today, these people live on *tortillas* (maize pancakes) and beans, in shacks made of adobe, reeds, and flattened tin cans. Their children are lucky to attend school, or to see the inside of a hospital if they are sick. Most homes have neither running water nor electricity. The poor are there to be used by the rich. There is even a Salvadoran term for them: *chusma*, meaning 'rabble' or 'garbage'.

The 20 rebellions since the Conquest were all put down savagely by the wealthy and their thugs, or by the army, to terrorise Salvadorans into acquiescence. In 1932, the military suppressed a rebellion in which *campesinos* (peasants) and Indians had killed about 150 people. In a week, they slaughtered 30,000 in *La Matanza*, or 'the killing', quelling dissent for three decades.

In the 1970s, the Catholic Church, in its 'option for the poor', began to support training, cooperatives, schools, and health centres. The effect was truly subversive. It made poor Salvadorans believe that they had rights, including the right to struggle for change. The FMLN had emerged from the 1970s, arguing that peaceful means of achieving justice were not viable in the face of electoral fraud and violent repression. By 1979, the human rights organisation Socorro Jurídico was documenting 1,000 killings a month. After the assassination of Archbishop Romero in March 1980, thousands joined the FMLN, and war broke out in the same year. The Sandinistas had just taken power in Nicaragua, and there was war in Guatemala. The Reagan Administration, reacting to these conflicts in the context of the Cold War, supported massive military and economic aid to the Salvadoran government, in its declared fight against international communism.

By 1981, the FMLN controlled much of El Salvador. The military responded with 'scorched earth' tactics, aiming to annihilate anyone who might support the FMLN, and to show what civilians risked if the guerrillas occupied an area where they lived. Non-combatants became military targets, and whole communities were wiped out. The population of Mozote was slaughtered in a day: more than 1,000 people, leaving only two survivors. At the Sumpul River, the military killed over 300 *campesinos* as they tried to reach safety in Honduras.

By 1983, international uproar over human-rights violations was immense. The government was losing the political battle. The USA advised a strategy of 'low-intensity conflict', though there was nothing low-intensity about its effect on civilians. The military began intensive bombing in the countryside. Civilians were turned over to ICRC or joined the 300,000 displaced in army-controlled camps.

With open dissent obliterated, the USA wanted to 'build a democracy' in El Salvador. Elections were held, with the Christian Democrat government heralding economic and agrarian reform, and a new constitution. However, the military remained unchallenged, and the underlying power structure untouched. Yet by 1986 people had begun to re-organise, and groups of displaced started to repopulate the conflict zones.

In November 1989, the FMLN launched a nationwide offensive, focusing on urban areas. Fighting began in 50 neighbourhoods of the capital, San Salvador. The military responded with ground troops, intense helicopter gunfire, and bombing. With no public transport and a strict curfew, church workers opened make-shift clinics for casualties who could not be evacuated. (The ICRC would not go to areas under fire without government permission.) The military raided these clinics, captured everyone, and shut down the facilities. In the capital alone, the death toll was estimated at 1,000 (mainly from the bombing), and some 30 offices of NGOs and community organisations were ransacked.

News was censored, though ex-Colonel Roberto D'Aubuisson went on the radio to identify 'terrorists', including the Jesuits from the Central American University (UCA). The armed forces detained anyone 'suspicious' — members of community organisations, NGO and church workers, politicians, professors, students. Leaflets urged Salvadorans to take up arms against 'the subversives', such as foreigners. After the Jesuits were murdered, a man stood outside the Archdiocese yelling through a bullhorn, 'The Jesuits are dead, now the other subversive priests will die'. Yet in spite of surveillance and death threats, the Archdiocese remained open.

Then UN-mediated negotiations began between the FMLN and the government, and a peace agreement was signed in January 1992. The war had caused dramatic social upheaval. One in five Salvadorans was displaced or outside the country. Almost 80,000 civilians had been killed or disappeared, many more tortured. Americas Watch estimates that over 90 per cent of the violations were committed by the armed forces or the death squads. The abuses have not been pursued through the courts. The military deny that most ever happened; the rich simply do not believe the statistics of brutality. These different perspectives on the war demonstrate the profound divisions in Salvadoran society.

Development and war

Poverty and marginalisation do not arise in a vacuum. To recognise injustice is to see that it is maintained by a distribution of power that perpetuates social and economic exclusion.

Addressing poverty means attacking its causes: development is about giving poor people access to the tools to change their situation. 'Empowerment' implies the power to bring about change, illustrated in the adage 'If you give people fish, they can eat one meal. If you teach them to fish, they can eat for a lifetime.' Education and technical training do confer some power, and that itself changes the *status quo*. But the question is: 'Who controls the pond in which the person is fishing?' People cannot challenge the injustice which causes their marginalisation unless they can change the balance of power which maintains it, as the following example shows.

In 1982, on the coast of Usulután, the FMLN drove a wealthy landowner off one of his properties, which produced cotton, grains, shrimp, and salt. The *hacienda* had functioned in a semi-feudal fashion, with *peons* working as serfs rather than wage-earners. Many of them later settled on the abandoned land as subsistence farmers. A co-operative federation helped them to get a bank loan to repair the salt-works, and production resumed in 1987. Heavy flooding damaged the works in 1988, and the co-operative sought funds to repair them again.

It was a good project. Displaced people were working together on the salt-works, while learning about community organisation in a project that could sustain them economically. An aid agency provided the funds, the repairs were done, the co-operative harvested a good quantity of high-grade salt, and representatives went to contact buyers and negotiate prices. They waited for them to collect the salt. After a few weeks the representatives went back to the buyers. They were told that the *hacienda* owner had sent word to all of them. He owned the only salt-bagging factory in the country and had declared that no-one purchasing salt from the co-operative could bag it there. He waited a few more weeks, until people were desperately short of cash and the loan payment was long overdue. He then offered 70 per cent of the market price. The alternative for the co-operative was to accede or watch the salt go to waste. The next year, the co-operative negotiated a good price with the buyers. When the *hacienda* owner saw that trucks were going to the cooperative, he got the military base nearby to station soldiers on the road and turn them back.

Such are the realities of supporting 'empowerment' in a society controlled by people determined to prevent change. In El Salvador, development work led inexorably to confrontation with powerful forces, implacably opposed to change.

State violence

The government relied on repression. People were kidnapped from their homes and disappeared. Some were tortured and killed, and their bodies left in public places. In Chalatenango, school children arrived one morning to find their teacher's head on her desk. Pedestrians were shot from passing vehicles, or homes were broken into and people shot at point-blank range. Men were rounded up and tortured in public. Women were raped before their families, girls were taken off to the barracks. Children were threatened in front of their parents, interrogated about them, or captured with them. Offices and homes were ransacked. People were followed and intimidated by phone or by letter, sometimes with death threats against them or a family member. Letters were opened, phones were tapped, military intelligence kept files on anyone 'suspicious', personal documents were constantly checked. International humanitarian workers were affected, as were their Salvadoran counterparts, who became the targets of repression. Between January and September 1989, people from 27 leading Salvadoran NGOs and community-based organisations were affected in the ways described above.

Counter-insurgency

Counter-insurgency is about militarising politics, and politicising the military. Humanitarian aid to the war-displaced becomes a military issue. In the words of General Waglestein of the US Southern Command: 'In a guerrilla war, the most important piece of territory is the six inches between a peasant's ears.' This denies poor people's right to think for themselves, hold their own opinions, opt for something, and build towards the future on that option. It implies that civilians must be under the control of one military group to prevent their co-option by the other. The assumption is that poor people can be controlled by cowing them with violence and forcing them to be dependent.

In El Salvador, anyone who resisted cooperating with the government authorities was assumed to be controlled by the FMLN. There was no middle ground. Debate and dissent were erased, as was the concept of neutrality. If an institution defined neutrality as independence from the government, it became suspect. When civilians stayed in a war zone, even if they did not take up arms, they were regarded as guerrillas. Any organisation that questioned the government was seen as subversive. In counter-insurgency, where the state must control everything, 'non-government' means 'anti-government'.

This polarised the world of humanitarian aid agencies. On one side were those organisations which insisted on their autonomy and were persecuted in the course of their work. On the other side were the civic-military action programmes supported by USAID and certain evangelical churches. The two sides disagreed in their analysis of the causes of the war, the problems posed by it, and the possible solutions to it. There was no common ground.

Humanitarian work took place in a context of indiscriminate bombing, civilian casualties, armed combat, economic sabotage, military road-blocks and searches, and all the scenery of war: barbed wire, checkpoints, tanks, bombers. Salvadorans were harassed, detained, killed; working with the victims exposed everyone to these risks. Neutrality was not merely questioned: its existence was denied.

Development became a question of defending the right to provide emergency assistance to anyone who needed it; to attend to the displaced independently of government control; to support civilians in their return to conflict areas and to remain there (as set out in the 1977 Protocol II of the Geneva Conventions, of which El Salvador is a signatory); to visit communities in the conflict zones who needed humanitarian assistance; to form or work for an NGO offering education and training to poor communities; to join or lead a popular organisation which could represent its members' interests; to be spared attack by the armed forces, whether as a beneficiary community, an NGO, or popular organisation.

Most experienced international aid agencies sought to share their thinking with their Salvadoran counterparts, and to respond quickly and creatively in emergencies. Given the need to understand the complexity of the situation, developing such trust was a priority that went beyond a bureaucratic or project-bound relationship. In El Salvador, it was called 'accompaniment', or travelling together.

Accompanying the repopulation movement

By 1985, 250,000 Salvadorans were displaced. Through the Archdiocese, a Salvadoran NGO (FUNDASAL) negotiated with the FMLN and the government an agreement to repopulate Tenancingo, a small town in a conflict zone. This had arguable success in terms of neutrality: the military occupied it in the morning, and the FMLN in the afternoon. The project was conceived without a deep understanding of the displaced, their various motivations and loyalties. Nonetheless, its impact was enormous. The conflict zones had been as inaccessible as the dark side of the moon. Almost overnight, Tenancingo made resettlement conceivable. This dramatically changed how the displaced saw their predicament, and they began to view internationally backed repopulation as the way forward.

In the same year, 'Operation Phoenix' was launched by the armed forces to clear civilians from the FMLN-held areas. Two thousand were taken off the Guazapa volcano alone. Such people were not going to kick their heels in a refugee camp. Soon, a committee of displaced held a national meeting, declaring that return to their places of origin — repopulation — was the only solution. In a bold move, protected by high-profile media coverage and foreign delegations, they led two returns from church-run camps back to conflict zones. Repopulation by a grassroots organisation had become a reality.

The subsequent repatriation of 4,500 refugees from Honduras, under the protection of the United Nations High Commissioner for Refugees (UNHCR), made it possible for international aid agencies and Salvadoran NGOs to work in the rural conflict zones. In addition, new groups were emerging in response to the repopulation movement and in the wake of the 1986 earthquake. NGOs, cooperatives, research institutes, and popular organisations began to open offices and claim their right to exist. Since counter-insurgency denied the space for discussion and debate, these groups were breaking public silence about the impact of the war on civilians.

Re-defining the conflict

The members of the repopulation movement claimed the right, backed by international humanitarian law, to be civilians in conflict areas. They refused to be victims. They won their right to return. With international involvement, indiscriminate bombing of the countryside was no longer possible. In the midst of combat, communities were rebuilt, people began to reconstruct their lives, and their organisations grew in strength. They needed housing materials and tools, and help with subsistence. Organisational assistance, such as training in technical skills, leadership, and community health-care, came with time. The communities then needed funding for small regional coordination offices, and mules on which to travel.

Repopulation was a daily struggle, as was the provision of humanitarian assistance, when access for personnel, materials, and supplies was often blocked, and there were frequent attacks against NGOs and resettled communities.

■ **Access for personnel:** San José de las Flores was a repopulated community in Chalatenango, three hours' journey from San Salvador. To visit meant applying for a military permit two weeks ahead, with passport copies. If the safe conduct was granted, one would be stopped about an hour outside San Salvador, where soldiers radioed the next base and decided if they would honour the safe conduct. If so, one proceeded to El Paraiso, where the Colonel decided whether to let one through. If he did, one would go to the military headquarters in Chalatenango, where another Colonel would make his own decision. If he signed the permit, one would proceed towards San José de las Flores. The military at the checkpoint outside the provincial capital would decide whether to allow one farther. At each checkpoint there were arguments, with the military questioning the permit's validity, denying entrance, checking with other officers, querying the purpose of the visit, whom one would see, what one would do, whether or not they should come, whom one worked for, what the agency did in the country; all this was accompanied by car searches, endless scrutiny of documents, and so on.

■ **Access for supplies and materials:** This was a nightmare of red tape. A *campesino* who left a war zone to sell his produce would use the opportunity to purchase domestic supplies. To take a box of matches, a candle, or a pound of beans back home, he needed a written permit from the officer in charge of the barracks. The loads of lumber, tools, and fertiliser for aid projects were often held up for days. Communities had to send delegations to the barracks and stage public protests to get these through. For instance, women made the seven-hour hike from their homes in the conflict zones of Morazán every week for two months, each time to request that the colonel permit two trucks of milk, flour, and sugar — supplies for schoolchildren sent by the Archdiocese — to be let through the checkpoint. Eventually, the colonel relented and the trucks went through.

■ **Attacks on NGOs and resettlements:** Meeting with a US church delegation, the Colonel in Chalatenango gestured towards the conflict zone, where about 29,000 civilians were recognised beneficiaries of various agencies (including UNHCR) and said, 'There isn't a civilian here, they are all guerrillas.' Classifying civilians as guerrillas meant that the military could persecute them. They would bomb, mortar, and aim rockets around and even within the settlements. Patrols would kill people who were alone, or throw grenades into the communities. Soldiers would destroy crops and animals, or set up camps nearby, so that farmers would be too frightened to tend their fields.

Yet people were going back. The repopulation movement was dynamic: it had a national platform, but was built on local organisation. It provided a concrete solution to displacement. It was empowering — an opportunity to try out new structures of authority and social organisation.

Aid agencies in war: compromise and commitment

Working in a war is determined by intangible realities that pose real questions for international aid agencies. In El Salvador, a network of silent rules thus conditioned how one behaved, with whom one was seen, what was said.

A Salvadoran friend once observed, 'The biggest problem is that people think that the war began when they came to El Salvador'. It can be hard to remember that there is an invisible web of history behind everything and everyone. One might deal with someone as an NGO worker, but know nothing of his past as a student leader ... that he was tortured ... that he was unsure whether he had said something that caused them to capture and kill his best friend ... that someone else was captured with him and released suspiciously soon ... that his sister was with the FMLN. There were reasons why people could not work together, or why something could only be done by one individual — reasons that were invisible.

A civil war is intimate: everyone knows everyone. To ousiders, the FMLN were an anonymous group; but to Salvadorans they were brothers, sisters, cousins, workmates, school friends, sons and daughters of neighbours. Almost none of this could be articulated. A major part of people's lives was lived below the surface: someone could be in a meeting, having just heard that a relative had been killed, and there was no way to express it. For an outsider, it was vital to be aware of how much one did not (and could not) know.

The civil war was a long and complicated process. While an outsider can learn to contribute, the learning never stops. There are major differences in culture and life experience between a Salvadoran and an outsider. No gulf can be bridged by denying it. Many aid workers are, like me, white, university-educated, middle-class people with good intentions and progressive politics. Our lives do not prepare us to speak the same language or share the world-view of a Salvadoran *campesino* at the opposite end of the power structure, who has grown up in poverty, been treated as worthless, and experienced repression as part of daily life.[3]

Foreigners were often troubled by the aggression with which popular organisations voiced their protests. One agency worker asked, 'Must they always make such a point of calling the military "assassins"?' Such 'belligerence' in fact derived largely from people's experience of oppression, and the denial of justice for their suffering. One's understanding of this largely unwritten history came through long talks at night with *campesinos*, or from odd scraps of time spent together with poor families. Their history told of their dehumanisation in a society that insisted they had no rights, and their awakening to the truth that they did have rights—but must struggle for them. So for people to raise their voices in protest was the clearest way to affirm their own humanity. It was a right they had won. It affirmed their experience, in a context that denied it; and, in the absence of justice, it was a public record of this truth.

To survive, people spoke in codes. Those who sought safety in the anonymity of the city had to invent new stories for themselves — where they came from, who they were—to conceal their origins. In Tenancingo, for example, were people with sympathies on both sides, for whom survival was paramount. The women with whom I worked had all lost one or more relatives, 90 per cent of them to the military and the death squads. Gradually, each of them told me her story, one by one. What surprised me was that their accounts were almost identical, and yet when I asked who the killers were, they would say, 'men who came in the night, we don't know' or 'the guerrillas'. This did not make sense. I got them to repeat their accounts, and tried to listen with 'a third ear'. Then I realised that they used almost ritual words and phrases, about the reaction of the dogs, the fear they felt before it happened, how the men entered their houses in the night. These were codes. They were trying to tell me, by including certain details (obvious to a Salvadoran *campesino*), that it was the military or the death squads who had killed their loved ones.

I was acutely aware of the delicate web of communication upon which people's safety rested. We foreigners blundered around, unused to having to disguise our feelings and re-write our past, just in order to survive. One had to listen hard to what was not said. As agency workers we want people to behave according to our cultural expectations, to tell us the straight truth, so that we can trust them. But to people who are trying to survive, that is a luxury they cannot afford. For them, 'talking straight' was not a bridge towards trust, but an unnecessary risk. People's loyalties in a war are complex. Their first obligation is not to outsiders, with little or no real involvement in a process which has caused so much loss of life. Aid workers see that their idea of being 'straight' comes from a particular political culture and context. They must respect people's caution, and listen to what they cannot put into words.

Repression and counter-insurgency create a situation that is anything but transparent. An aid agency may demand complete transparency, but it is demanding the impossible. Many Salvadorans were trying to function in a civil war, having seen people killed or tortured for doing what was now classified as subversive. They were not just surviving: they were working to break the cycle of violence. For some, that meant political commitment to the FMLN; to others it meant opposition to the government. Counter-insurgency aims to deny people the right to an independent political viewpoint. Individuals felt profoundly their right to have their own opinions.

Transparency is also affected by the way in which everyday life is politicised by war. In El Salvador, the key was to carry out legitimate humanitarian work *within* a politicised reality, rather than seeking a (non-existent) 'non-political' space. This was demonstrated in the reaction to President Duarte's attempt in 1987 to impose daylight-saving time. Because the clocks were brought forward an hour, *campesinos* had to wake up in the dark. They took it as another sign of the government's deception. People began to distinguish between 'Duarte time' and 'old time', and set their watches accordingly. Buses were routinely stopped and soldiers checked passengers' watches to find out who was disloyal to the government. Where is the non-political space, when even asking the time is politically charged?

Transparency and accountability and are not always synonymous. Accountability means ensuring that people receive what they are due, even in conflict zones. However, for about six years it was impossible to visit these areas safely, and so most aid agencies had to rely on third-party accounts of the situation facing civilians.

Commitment: how far does this take us?

We faced this question daily. International agencies give people resources to help them to change their situation. They decide to work for change, and we support them. But the issue does not end there. Their decision often puts our 'partners' in danger. In a counter-insurgency war, assistance which helps people to work for change may turn them into targets.

For example, a grassroots organisation in a conflict zone received support for a training course, after which one participant was picked up by the military on his way home and tortured, because they discovered that he was learning leadership skills.

In another instance, so many promoters from poor urban communities were being captured that one NGO devoted a training session to the best way to respond if this happened. Acting out being picked up by the military, they had someone on the floor and two people 'beating' him with sticks, shouting questions. One was, 'Who gives you the money to do this work? Which agency is it?'

There are no easy answers. People decide to take the risks, but our support implicates us. We do not take the same risks. But what is our commitment to the people we support when their work for change brings them into such situations?

In such a context, it was impossible to know if something one did, or said, or was overheard saying, could endanger another. For example, during the 1989 offensive, I went with a colleague to check the offices of various community organisations, seeking ways to distribute emergency assistance. Only one was occupied. We had a quick talk with the people there and fixed a meeting for later in the day. They never arrived: two hours later, the military rounded up everyone, including a man and his two-year old son. The child was left in a cell while his father was tortured. Part of the torture was listening to the screams of a child they said was his son. In fact, it was a recording, and the boy was left alone, terrified, hungry, and thirsty, but not beaten. Who knows what damage was done to those two people? What the father said about someone else, to make them stop torturing his son? What the child will remember of the time when his father left him alone in that terrible place?

One can go over and over such an event. Was the raid planned, or did the visit of two foreigners draw attention to the office? Should I have telephoned, not visited? It is impossible to know, so it remains a hard question. It highlights the ethical dilemmas of supporting people — our 'partners' — whose work puts them in danger, but from our privileged position of safety. Perhaps all one can do is work to end the repression, and to react swiftly when someone is threatened.

Empowerment in practice

The wartime structures of NGOs and popular organisations were often rigid and hierarchical, but made up of highly creative and dedicated individuals. Working under perpetual siege, these organisations needed cohesion, which often led to top-down decision-making. In supporting Salvadorans to remove the causes of their exclusion, the challenge was to help them move from being war victims to becoming development actors, even in a context of war.

Some refugees had almost a decade of collective experience in Honduras, which gave them the basis for analysing the world, questioning their situation, and taking action. Discussing empowerment in ways that could eventually apply to their own organisational structures, we would ask what opportunity was built into their work for reflection and analysis of their own experiences; we encouraged them to consider the role of collective organisation and to examine their own decision-making structures and local distribution mechanisms. We would examine together the ultimate objective of the activity or organisation, as well as its relationship with marginalised community members; and look for any potential for education and leadership training. We would also try to check that people at the grassroots shared the same concepts as the NGO working with them. We did not always get satisfactory answers, and groups were sometimes given seed money to see how they developed. Subsequent dialogue would help us come to a better common understanding.

From victim to actor

The people who returned to the conflict zones had experienced the war first-hand. They were the survivors of massacres, people who had suffered atrociously at the hands of the military, who had seen children hung from rafters and bayoneted, or hurled against trees. Yet these were the people who went back to their homes.

Largely deserted, the conflict zones were cut off from the rest of the country, with no commerce, the roads overgrown, and no public or social services of any kind. People had to rebuild homes, clear fields, and just do whatever they could. In doing so, their confidence grew. They began to feel that they had rights, and saw that there was international interest in violations of human rights in their country.

To survive, civilians needed supplies, guarantees of physical security, and respect for human rights. They gradually began to stand up to the military. They made good use of the presence of international observers, and gradually gained the confidence to issue appeals to UNHCR and to report and publicly denounce abuses. Campesinos who had recently been hounded through the mountains by his troops would form delegations to visit the local Colonel and demand their rights.

In Santa Marta, Cabañas, 300 people walked 20 kilometres from their repatriated settlement to the provincial capital and stood outside the barracks for three days until the Colonel agreed to let through the trucks of fertiliser he had detained.

In Segundo Montes, Morazán, after the military had killed over 500 chickens in a poultry farm belonging to this major resettlement, community members loaded the dead chickens into pick-up trucks, drove to the provincial capital, and dumped them in front of the barracks.

In Guarjila, Chalatenango, where 1,100 people had resettled themselves, the military demanded that they turn over their leaders. The people stood together and claimed 'We are all leaders. If you take one, you take us all.' The military could not single out one individual. It is hard to appreciate the impact of these acts in a society where all protest had been silenced. More amazingly, the actors were *campesinos* who had directly experienced violence, and so knew the price of what they were doing.

Some accused the FMLN of forcing people to live in the conflict zones, still seeing *campesinos* as fodder for one side or the other. But people cannot be manipulated to take such risks and continually face that kind of danger. They were standing up to the military in the midst of a war, despite the continued abuses of human rights. Having won several small victories, they began to believe that they too had a measure of power.

An incident in San José de las Flores illustrates this power in action. The square was full of visitors and journalists, commemorating the anniversary of the repopulation and waiting for the Bishop to celebrate mass. Without warning, the Atlacatl Battalion arrived and began an altercation. Community members told them to leave. In response, the soldiers raised their guns and shot over the heads of people by the church and then at their feet. In one spontaneous surge, the townspeople rushed the soldiers, who turned and ran, lobbing tear-gas grenades behind them. The unarmed population literally ran them out.

The repopulated communities began to realise their own dignity and power in a process of transformation that was hard to stop. They had some support, but most importantly they had some success. They realised that the powerful did not always win, and that they had important weapons themselves. Their relationship to power was changing. The rediscovery of their own humanity became part of their struggle.

Some may say, 'No, the government saw these resettlements as dangerous because they were secret supporters of the FMLN'. I think not. Repopulation solved some of the problems of displacement, and may have benefited the FMLN to an extent. More significantly, what was happening was carefully watched by other *campesinos*. As a man from a community under military control said, 'You know, when people from La Virtud [a resettlement] were invaded by the military, they ran like animals. They hid in caves, they lost everything, the military killed everyone they could find. Those people were worse than animals. But now, they have come back; they have schools, a clinic, they are planting their fields, and the military can't stop them! But here, we're as wretched as when the war started.'

A breakthrough took place when people who were victims and excluded began to organise and gain ground. They began to see the relationship between themselves and power in a new way. This is why the ruling classes saw them as dangerous (and ultimately more threatening than a guerrilla movement), for they no longer wanted to play their part as the marginalised.

Oppression in El Salvador depended on the majority living in fear. When people lose their fear, the whole structure begins to creak. Development depends on two things: oppressed people need to change their own perceptions of their relationship to power, and there have to be real structural changes. The repopulation movement brought these elements together, which is why it threatened the *status quo*.

After experiencing their wartime courage and hope, it is sad that, in peacetime, the repopulated communities have been unable to build on what they initiated. They have failed to move from the rigidity of wartime community structures and practices to more open, democratic ones, and other powerful and monied interests have chipped away at their unity. They have been unable to assert their demands within the FMLN agenda, and the FMLN leadership has not prioritised their development needs. Despite this, the historic breakthrough in poor people's vision of themselves must one day find a new expression.

Note

Many former colleagues have commented on earlier drafts of this paper, but the views expressed are mine alone, and cannot be attributed to any of the international aid agencies for whom I worked in Central America.

■ **Martha Thompson,** *who trained in public health, has lived in Latin America and the Caribbean since 1979. She began working with Salvadoran refugees in the early 1980s, initially for Concern and later for Catholic Relief Services (CRS) both in Honduras and in El Salvador. After a secondment to FUNDASAL, the Salvadoran NGO running the Tenancingo repopulation project, she joined Oxfam UK/I as its El Salvador Programme Officer, and later worked as the Deputy Representative. After this, she became a resident adviser to the refugee return programme in Guatemala, leaving in 1995 to take up her current post as Oxfam Canada's Programme Development Officer for Cuba and the Eastern Caribbean, based in Havana.*

This paper was first published in Development in Practice *Volume 6, Number 4, in 1996.*

The global struggle for the right to a place to live

Miloon Kothari

Introduction[1]

At the end of the twentieth century, injustice, exclusion, and dispossession prevail all over the world on an unprecedented scale. One aspect of this state of affairs which has received insufficient attention is the struggle of people and communities existing in inadequate housing and living conditions. Related to this is the growing incidence of people and communities facing evictions from their homes and lands, whether for economic reasons, or because of environmental degradation, or because of conflict over land rights.

This article is a preliminary attempt to represent the insights gained by a global organisation, Habitat International Coalition (HIC), in its efforts to come to terms with the enormity of the challenge that faces local, national, and international organisations which are attempting to alter the stark reality of the lives of millions of people who are forced to exist in inadequate housing and living conditions.

The numbers are sobering. Close to 1.2 billion people, almost one quarter of the world's population, survive in housing and living conditions that are unhealthy and precarious, including more than 100 million who are completely homeless.

HIC is a global movement of grassroots organisations, community-based organisations (CBOs), and non-government organisations (NGOs) from 70 countries, working on a range of issues stemming from the struggle for the right of everyone to a place in which to live in peace and dignity. Groups working on human settlements, women's rights to land and inheritance, children's rights, land rights, environment, evictions and displacement, and human rights form the membership of HIC.

In attempting to tackle the immense problems of poor housing worldwide, HIC has adopted a perspective which is based on human rights. Such a holistic approach, rooted in the dignity of the individual and the collective identity of the community, is necessary because the current assault on the space and place where people live their lives is multi-dimensional. This assault not only threatens the house, the four walls, and the roof, but — through targeting the home — it undermines life itself. It violates the basic right to a place to live, and the basic right of people and communities to gain and sustain an adequate standard of living.

All people and communities have a right to a place to live: a basic right to live in security and with dignity. Taking this as a point of departure is an invaluable first step, as such an approach serves to root the debate in the day-to-day reality of the struggle for survival and livelihood rights, as well as for somewhere to live.

One definition of this holistic concept states that *'the human right to adequate housing is the right of every woman, man and child to gain and sustain a secure home and community in which to live in peace and dignity'.*[2] Encompassed within this are numerous elements of the right to housing. They include the following entitlements:

- the right to security of tenure, assuring the right to reside and settle;
- the right not to be dispossessed from one's home and surroundings;
- the right to resettle for communities living in health-threatening environments;
- the right of equal access to civic services;
- the right to natural resources;
- the right to a healthy and safe environment;
- the right to housing finance;
- the right to self-expression in all housing activity;
- the right to form local CBOs and to control the production, distribution, and regeneration of housing resources;
- the right of gender equality in all dimensions of the housing process outlined above.

These core components stem from inviolable principles which are based on overriding respect for the inherent dignity of the individual and the collective identity of the community. These principles are the rule of law; equality and non-discrimination; self-determination; the right to information; the right to a healthy living environment; democratic participation; equality in land relations; gender equality; economic parity; the maintenance of cultural identity; and skills and the role of the government.[3]

In the current crisis in the state of housing, land, and living conditions, all of these principles are compromised. It is important to understand the enormity of the crisis and the consequences being faced by women, men, young people, children, and whole communities worldwide.

Measures which promote exclusion and violence

In grappling with the worldwide crisis of inadequate housing and living conditions, we have identified certain phenomena whose prevalence contributes to the dire situation in which poor people find themselves today. Everywhere, the forces affecting all those struggling for a place to live are strikingly similar.

These common dimensions point to a lack of governance and a severe abrogation of government obligations to promote and protect citizens' housing rights and human rights. Cumulatively the continued prevalence of these phenomena points to a failure of governance which leads to exclusion, dispossession, and violence becoming endemic in societies. This absolute failure of governance has also led, in various countries, to the institutionalisation of insecure and inadequate housing and living conditions. Some of the most common abuses are described below.

■ *Insecurity of home, land, and person*: public authorities are unwilling to give security of tenure to residents forced by circumstances to live without title; they fail to give direct protection to tenants who are at the mercy of landlords; they fail to protect residents from forced evictions.

■ *The misuse of planning mechanisms*: regional plans and city-development plans often discriminate against the poor; government authorities manipulate planning mechanisms and instruments to further their aims (or the aims of the forces with which they are in collusion, such as land developers or politicians) to achieve either the objective of clearing land for speculative purposes, or the aim of segregating different ethnic and economic groups.

■ *The abuse of law*: laws are passed which contain loopholes and are open to misuse; where effective legislation exists to protect the rights of the majority of residents, it is often not implemented; laws to protect tenants and control rents are often diluted and in many cases dismantled.

■ *The denial of essential civic services* (potable water, electricity, sanitation, and so forth).

■ *Inability to control market forces*: State authorities fail to control the ravages of unbridled land speculation, thereby forcing people to live in increasingly marginal and unhealthy areas.

■ *The prevalence of forced evictions*: governments fail to control the conditions which lead to forced evictions: increases in unemployment; changes in modes of agricultural production, particularly affecting small farmers and rural workers; intensified extraction of natural resources to fuel foreign trade; overall reductions in purchasing power, due to the fall in real wages and the rise in the costs of basic necessities; the tendency towards market-based policies controlling private-sector housing and land development, and corresponding increases in land and housing prices. When forced evictions take place, the agents of the State (police, demolition task forces, etc.) often collude with land-owners, permitting the use of direct violence and even contributing to the brutality.

■ *The integration of national economies into global economies*: predominant neo-liberal ideology calls for a reduction in State subsidies and controls on the land and housing sector; this leads to the lifting of restrictions on market forces, leaving the pricing of land and housing resources to the whims of the market and the demands of the profit-taker; housing is reduced to the status of a commodity to be bought and sold; the State withdraws from spending on social sectors such as housing; it dismantles welfare provisions which should protect people's access to housing and land; and retreats from its role of guaranteeing conditions for access to housing and land and improvement of living conditions.

■ *The loss of common-property resources*: the failure of States to recognise the importance of common-property resources in both urban and rural areas leads to the demise of the institutions and the cultural patterns which used to protect and sustain these resources; in turn this leads to the destruction of the natural-resource base and the common-property resources upon which local rural economies depend, through changes in land-tenure systems (the removal of protective legal measures, etc.); through changes in agricultural systems; and through the undermining of local economies, skills, and identity.

■ *The creation of ethnic and economic ghettos*: governments fail to prevent (and in many cases collude in creating) the segregation of different ethnic groups and economic classes in cities, towns, and villages.

■ *Non-compliance with national and international legal human-rights instruments*: States across the world abrogate their constitutional duties and the human-rights obligations under international law which protect housing and land rights; they fail to reconcile the often contradictory obligations imposed by trade treaties, debt agreements, and structural adjustment policies with human-rights obligations.

Consequences of measures which promote exclusion and violence

The phenomena outlined above are not a comprehensive listing, but an indication of the range of forces which must be tackled in any attempt to contribute to lasting change such that people and communities have the human right to a secure place to live. These phenomena need to be viewed as debilitating factors which further inhibit any efforts to sustain change.

The persistence and consolidation of these forces lead to only one conclusion: that inadequate and insecure housing and living conditions are becoming a pernicious reality of contemporary urban and rural life; and, more disturbingly, that the existence of inadequate living conditions has become institutionalised. Instead of protecting and promoting the interests of the poor, the role of relevant institutions has become to act as pawns in the hands of the wealthier sections of society who, unsatisfied with lavish lifestyles and disproportionate hoarding of resources and money, are out to acquire yet more land, more resources, and more material goods, and have become addicted to the accumulation of material wealth. For poor people and communities struggling to survive, the cost is devastating.

The following points summarise the impact on people and communities of the institutionalisation of inadequate and insecure housing and living conditions, and the failure of governance.

■ *The impact of the creation of insecurity of home, land and person*: there are severe psychological consequences for people who are forced to live in daily fear of evictions; communities who are hard put to defend and organise for their rights are often incapacitated by the harsh conditions in which they have to struggle for a secure place to live.

■ *The impact of forced evictions and inadequate resettlement*: forced evictions lead to numerous consequences in both the short and long terms. The immediate consequences are threats to life, injuries, and deaths caused by violence during the evictions; damage to and destruction of homes; loss of land and affinity to land; the trauma of having to stay in temporary shelters or in a state of homelessness before resettlement; the impact on work and income; the particular trauma caused to women; a weakening of the coping capacity that is essential to the survival of the whole family; disruption of children's education; and increased incidence of mental illness. The long-term impacts are uprooting and dispossession; a decline in economic status; the loss of educational opportunities; and the destruction of family and community bonds.

■ *The marginalisation and alienation of the poor and the disadvantaged*: the capacities of already economically and ecologically vulnerable segments of society are weakened still further.

■ *The creation of ethnic conflict*: the constant reality of inadequate and insecure housing and living conditions is one aspect of the perpetuation of poverty which provides fertile ground for the breeding of ethnic, racial, and class conflict, and provides a reservoir for the fomenting of violence that is often the result of such conflict.

■ *The creation of landlessness and homelessness*: States fail to recognise the fact that, particularly for millions of people living in rural areas (indigenous and tribal people, marginal farmers, rural agricultural labour), land is the principal resource for survival. Governments fail to adopt land reforms or implement existing statutes, and fail to arrest speculation and the commercialisation of land, which results today in a situation where landlessness and homelessness are on the increase.

■ *Decline in health conditions*: the quality of living conditions declines to life-threatening levels, as shown by a resulting rise in rates of child mortality and the incidence of communicable diseases.

■ *Impact on women*: all the above consequences affect women in particular. They face discrimination in all aspects of the right to land and housing: land security and the right to inherit land and property; access to credit facilities; access to information essential for participation in housing activities and in contributing to the improvement of the living environment; access to essential housing services and resources, including potable water, sanitation, fuel and fodder; and access to appropriate housing projects, up-grading schemes, and resettlement areas.

By their deliberate inattention to — and, at times, their direct involvement in — the consequences outlined above, governments are abetting the uprooting and further segregation of people and communities. It is necessary to assess the magnitude of loss to the inherent dignity of the individual and the collective identity of communities, and to understand these forces and consequences as widespread infringements of human rights.

Certain human rights are closely and indivisibly related to the right to housing and land rights, and are infringed upon as a result of both the forces responsible and the consequences outlined above. They include the right to health; the right to a safe environment; and the right to livelihood (work). Also important to maintaining the security of the home and land are the right to vote, the right to information, the right to gender equality, the right to freedom of movement and to choose one's residence, the right not to be arbitrarily deprived of property, and the right to non-discrimination.

A programme which tries to grapple with these realities must ensure that energies are spent first on analysing why positive change is not happening; and second on suggesting institutional development (of government and civil society) which will create lasting change and conditions of empowerment to sustain change.

The response of NGOs and civil society

In response to the dire reality of housing and living conditions across the world, the past ten years have seen the emergence of numerous national grassroots campaigns, networks, and movements working on the right to housing and campaigning against forced evictions. Significant initiatives have been taken in India, the Philippines, Colombia, Hong Kong, Canada, and Great Britain. More recently, campaigns on the right to housing and against evictions have emerged in Palestine, Israel, Panama, the Dominican Republic, and Brazil. There is also growing attention to the issue among coalitions of NGOs and CBOs in South Africa, the United States, Nigeria, Italy, Peru, France, Kenya, and Mexico.[4]

The activities of these campaigns and alliance-building initiatives have been diverse. Using the fundamental basis of the human right to adequate housing, their work has included popular processes of drafting housing-rights legislation (India, the Philippines); conceptual work on the content of the right to housing, incorporating learning from vernacular languages and local understanding of the right (India); launching a successful nationwide campaign to get the right to housing into the national constitution (Colombia); forming task forces of the urban poor to counter evictions (the Philippines, Brazil); collaboration on regional campaigns on urban land rights (Latin America and the Caribbean); preparing through popular processes alternative development plans to counter insensitive government master-plans (Israel); and preparing alternative reports for UN human-rights treaty bodies (the Philippines, the Dominican Republic, Panama, Canada, Italy, Israel, Palestine, Mexico). All these groups have also conducted information and awareness campaigns, through which they have attempted to mobilise national public opinion on the imperative of the human-rights approach to tackling housing and land issues.

Utilising the conceptual and practical basis of national and local-level housing-rights work and the wide-ranging legal recognition accorded to the right to housing in international human-rights law,[5] the last decade has also seen HIC initiating Global Campaigns for Housing Rights and against forced evictions. These campaigns have used international human-rights law as a basis for building public opinion at home. This has provided an additional instrument for mobilisation by local and national groups, working at various levels to devise pre-emptive strategies to halt evictions and gain housing rights.

The principal organ of HIC, charged with co-ordinating and providing guidance in all areas of work related to the right to housing and forced evictions, is its Housing Rights Committee (HRC). The HRC co-ordinates HIC's Global Campaign for the Right to Housing and its Global Campaign against Forced Evictions.

While the active work of the HRC since 1991 has involved various activities and programmes, such as assessment visits and fact-finding missions, work at the UN, publications work, and work on co-ordinating global NGO meetings, the current phase is leading more towards the development of a 'national focus programme'.

The HIC-HRC National Focus programme[6]

Since 1995, based on the lessons learned since 1991 and in order to meet more consistently the growing demands of local and national groups, the work of the HRC has taken on a more national focus. The main elements of the National Focus programme as they are being developed are as follows:

a. *Training at local and national levels*: the HRC can draw upon the wide experience of the various HIC Committees and Working Groups (Women and Shelter, Housing Rights, Finance, Housing and Environment) and members of HIC to provide training on the following aspects of the right to housing:

- campaigning: how to campaign effectively, both locally and nationally; how to ensure and retain involvement in grassroots groups; how to link national, regional, and international campaigning; how to mobilise against forced evictions;[7]
- women's rights and children's rights: mobilising for women's rights to housing, inheritance, and land, and for more effective leadership and participation in mobilisation and monitoring on these issues;
- research and documentation, including report-writing and data-collection;

- legal activism: learning how communities have handled legal-aid test cases; developing legal arguments using national and international law; studying actions possible outside courts and lessons to be learned from precedents set in housing-rights struggles in other parts of the world;

- the United Nations system: how to make effective use of the UN human-rights system; the lessons learned by groups from other countries in utilising the UN system;[8]

- community finance: techniques for self-sufficiency; strategies for raising community finance which have worked elsewhere;

- fund-raising for NGO and CBO housing-rights work: public and private funding, through subscriptions and strategies for procuring urgently needed funds;

- up-grading of living conditions and the use of appropriate building materials: how to prepare rapid surveys of housing and living conditions and skeleton plans for village up-grading;

- alternative planning strategies: how to prepare alternative master and regional plans;

- strategies for the regularisation of land: how to gain security of tenure; how to gain regularisation of land and property through, for example, building cooperative housing.

b. *Lobbying and advocacy work at the UN*: once information has been received from local and national groups, or if a country has been identified for a National Focus programme, the work at the UN in Geneva can include the following components:

- assisting in identifying the appropriate UN body to present testimony on local and national situations and ensuring grassroots participation at these sessions;

- conducting training in the use of international human-rights law and UN bodies to promote the right to housing in local and national conditions;

- assistance in the preparation of alternative reports to the relevant UN bodies;

- assisting in the preparation of oral and written statements on the state of local housing and land issues to the relevant UN bodies; and

- introduction to other international organisations working at the UN which can also assist local and national organisations in their human-rights work.

c. *Regular visits and consultations*: designated HRC members will make six-monthly visits to a country with a National Focus programme. These visits are useful for maintaining constant contact with the local groups and for developing, in collaboration with the groups, relevant aspects of the programme.

d. *Fact-finding missions*: once a country has been identified for a National Focus programme, the HRC can upon request co-ordinate targeted fact-finding missions which concentrate on the situation in particular areas of a National Focus country to determine the state of housing and living conditions or the situation regarding forced evictions.

e. *Exchange programmes*: the HRC can co-ordinate exchange programmes between activists from National Focus countries or between a country with a Programme and one that is under consideration for one. These visits can be useful to share strategies and to learn from each other's experiences.

f. *Solidarity work*: the HRC can provide a platform for solidarity work between groups from different National Focus countries to come together to share experiences and strategies. Such solidarity can then lead to exchange programmes and more targeted work within the UN human-rights programme. (In June 1996, for example, during the Habitat II Conference in Istanbul, the HRC organised a Solidarity Workshop between Palestinians, Tibetans, and Kurds.)

g. *Urgent actions*: if necessary, the HRC can initiate urgent actions, using the networks of HIC and COHRE (Centre on Housing Rights and Evictions), on situations requiring rapid action at the international level. The HRC can also collaborate with international organisations which are working in the same countries on related issues. (Recently the HRC has collaborated with FIAN, the international alliance on the right to food and land rights, on urgent actions in response to eviction cases in Brazil and Occupied Palestine.)

HRC's legal work at the UN

In addition to the lobbying and representational work of the HRC at the UN, the HRC, alongside HIC's affiliate COHRE, has, as part of the HIC Global Campaigns, also pursued intensive legal work within the UN human-rights programme to promote UN action on the right to housing and against forced evictions. This work has been responsible for and contributed to the following developments:

- The appointment of a UN Special Rapporteur on the Right to Adequate Housing: Justice Rajindar Sachar of India. HIC and COHRE also worked very closely with the Special Rapporteur in the preparation of his four reports.[9]

- The adoption by the UN Commission on Human Rights and the UN Sub-Commission on the Prevention of Discrimination and the Protection of Minorities of resolutions declaring that forced evictions are a gross violation of human rights.[10]

- The adoption by the UN Committee on Economic, Social and Cultural Rights of a General Comment on the right to adequate housing. This General Comment is a legal interpretation of the article of the UN Covenant on Economic, Social and Cultural Rights that contains the right to housing.[11]

- An active role, in collaboration with local and national groups, to get the UN Committee on Economic, Social and Cultural Rights to cite the Dominican Republic and Panama as having been in violation of the Covenant on Economic, Social and Cultural Rights on account of their practice of large-scale evictions.[12]

It is also important, for the theme of this article, that most of the legal work at the UN has relied for its conceptual and substantive understanding of the right to housing and the phenomenon of forced evictions on the knowledge and understanding of grassroots organisations from across the world. This is largely a result of the co-ordinating work which HIC has done in presenting these voices to the UN.

Lessons from the work: sustaining change

What have been the advantages of international work to promote and sustain change? What has contributed to harmonious and effective collaboration between local, national, regional, and international levels? Some of the main elements are listed below.

a. *The formation of campaigns*: the HRC has played, based on the trust gained through sustained work, a catalytic role in promoting national campaigns on the right to housing and against forced evictions. Once the campaigns have been formed, the HRC has worked alongside these groups to develop the National Focus programme, as described above. Recent examples are the Palestine Housing Rights Movement (PHRM) in Israeli-occupied Palestine and autonomous Palestine, and the Arab Co-ordinating Committee for Housing Rights in Israel (ACCHRI).

b. *Assessment visits*: the HRC has found it helpful to conduct assessment visits to different countries. These have been useful for determining the nature of NGO activity on the issues of housing and living conditions; and the views of local and national civil-society groups on the need for solidarity work with HIC. The visits have established contacts with NGOs and prompted the collection of information to assist the preparation of fact-finding missions (as in the cases of Turkey, Palestine, Israel, and Brazil).

c. *Fact-finding missions*: the HRC continues to conduct fact-finding missions to determine the state of housing and living conditions and to report on the situation regarding forced evictions. These missions, and the co-ordination required from local organisations to plan them, have also contributed to identifying the need for National Focus programmes (as in the cases of Dominican Republic, Palestine, Israel, Brazil, and Turkey).

d. *Work at the United Nations*: the HRSC work at the UN has involved the active participation of local groups with whom HIC is in contact. This participation has included testifying before UN bodies and preparing alternative reports. The preparation of these reports has often involved the coming together of various local and national groups. The network thus established has continued work at the national level in mobilising on the right to housing and in monitoring how the respective governments are complying with their obligations on the right to housing under international human-rights instruments (see, for example, Mexico, Panama, and Israel).

e. *Global meetings*: several global meetings, from the sessions of the HRSC meetings to Conferences like Habitat II, have promoted the need for national-level work. In some cases, representatives of local groups have been influenced by exposure at these meetings to consider the possibilities of linking national and international work, and are attempting in their countries to form coalitions and campaigns (as in the cases of Brazil, Peru, and the United States).

f. *Development of principles for global work*: by learning from local and national work and by utilising the human-rights basis of the HIC Global Campaigns on the right to housing and against forced evictions, the HIC-HRC has evolved a set of principles which guide its work with local and national civil-society organisations. The principles are these:

- to work primarily with a coalition, campaign, or network of civil-society organisations and not with individual organisations;

- to initiate activities in a country only if requested to do so by local or national groupings of organisations;
- to undertake activities (assessment visits, fact-finding missions, training) only if HIC determines that it has the capacity to continue work in that country;
- to work towards developing a National Focus programme in these countries;
- to move towards, over time, the integration of representatives of groupings of organisations, from countries where HIC has formed a national focus, into the decision-making body such as the HIC-HRC.

The main areas of work outlined above have resulted in several changes that have been of direct benefit to local and national groups. First, they have created local expertise: the consistent work in these countries, involving the formation of campaigns, fact-finding missions, UN work, and participation at global meetings, has helped to create local expertise in areas such as the conceptual and practical contents of the right to housing and land, research and documentation in the field, and the use of international human-rights law and the UN system.

Secondly, they have encouraged wider participation in international decision making: the development of a focus at the national level has also contributed to a change in composition of the HRSC, such that now the membership consists of more and more grassroots individuals, representing groups who are campaigning for housing rights and against forced evictions in their countries. Thus, in addition to the development of work at the national levels, local organisations are now also able to contribute at the international level to decision-making on issues with which the HRC deals.

Third, they have helped to overcome local and national conflicts between civil-society organisations: we have found that having an external focus, such as the need for the preparation of alternative reports and testimony for UN human-rights bodies, brings together previously incompatible organisations. Combined with the mediating role which HIC has played at the local levels, this has led to the groups' staying together and developing further work (as in the cases of Israel, Mexico, and Panama).

Fourth, numerous advantages have been gained as a result of the platform which the HIC-HRC has been able to provide at global meetings to promote solidarity work. These include opportunities to spread the knowledge of local situations to groups from different countries; getting support in the form of letters and faxes for urgent cases; the possibility of exchange visits to learn from those who live in similar conditions; and sharing strategies of work at international forums such as the UN human-rights bodies.

Looking ahead: future challenges

The work on the ground and at the UN, in particular over the past six years, indicates the requirements that are necessary to sustain change. There are many lessons which can be derived from the work outlined above on the rights to housing and land. These are the lessons from the work that HIC has been directly involved in and the work of groups working independently at local, national, and regional levels. Taking those into account, and keeping in mind the need to surmount the obstacles elaborated earlier, we can identify the following challenges that must be built upon to set positive change on a firm footing.

For groups at all levels, including governmental bodies, who are involved in legal, policy, and mobilising work, it is imperative to use as a guidepost the principles contained in international human-rights law: non-discrimination, self-determination, the rule of law, equality.[13] The adoption in practice of these inviolable principles and the respect for human rights which they call for is essential for sustaining change. The respect, in turn, for the right to housing and land is imperative to be able to counter the market-dominated policy directives to which land and housing have become hostage today.

First, it is especially critical to stress the role of human rights as a means of both empowering people and communities, and of holding States accountable: of transforming the internal structure of the States through the empowering of the civil society. Simultaneously, we must stress that social policies at national levels need to be developed which recognise the primacy of human rights and their 'empowering' dimensions.

Second, it is also important to participate in evolving mechanisms such that the non-State actors (such as the international financial institutions and transnational corporations) can be held accountable to the principles and the obligations contained in international human-rights law.

Third, it is vital to use the UN system. More groups need to be informed about the possibilities of using the UN treaty-body mechanisms. There is a need to encourage the preparation of parallel reports by NGOs working at the local and national levels, to provide a mechanism through which NGOs can participate at the UN, and to evolve a means through which local and national civil-society organisations can take part in exposing the records of their governments and in offering their own solutions, such as alternative development plans, to the problems they face.

There is a need also for local and national groups to hold their governments accountable to their obligations under the international human-rights treaties which they have ratified, and the relevant international plans of actions to which they have agreed. For the groups working on housing and land rights, it is critical that they attempt to hold their governments accountable, for example, to the provisions on the right to housing and land contained in the Global Plan of Action adopted in June 1996 at Istanbul at the World Conference on Human Settlements (Habitat II).

Fourth, we need to deepen our work on housing and land rights. At a critical and more ambitious level, we need to develop a comprehensive treatment of the right to housing and land rights which brings out all the dimensions of land and housing issues. It is only through such a detailed approach that these inviolable rights will figure in the work of a wider spectrum of individuals and institutions at local, regional, and international levels. Many of these entities are already dealing with the issues contained in, and the action indicated by, the formulation of 'the right to a place to live in peace, security and dignity'. A more direct human-rights approach can, we feel, provide for a sharper critique of government responsibility and more clues towards interventions necessary by all sectors of society to promote and act upon empowerment of traditionally marginalised and discriminated communities.

Fifth, there is a need to strengthen local and international work. As this article has tried to demonstrate, there are numerous benefits which can accrue from local and national groups collaborating with international organisations. These benefits are even more likely if campaigning and mobilisational capacities are increased at all levels. It is also important for international organisations, once trust has been gained, to play the mediating role between local and national organisations, so that political and ideological differences can be overcome, especially if the aim of all concerned is to promote and defend the human right to adequate housing, including devising means to confront evictions.

It is also critically important for international organisations to develop intensive programmes of work, even in a few countries. We have developed 'national focus' programmes as described above; these have proved to be fundamental to the consistent development of substantive and comprehensive work on the right to housing. The aspect of training, in full collaboration with local and national groups, on all aspects of the right to housing and land rights has been particularly beneficial and continues to be the main demand from the groups that initiate work with us.

This paper has described the forces which continue to cause the crisis in housing and land issues across the world. It has also described attempts to respond to this crisis, as well as the lessons learned and clues discerned for promoting solidarity, justice, and change. The forces and the consequences they unleash on people and communities against positive change are overwhelming. The only way forward is to keep trying, to build upon the work already done and the lessons already learned, so that we may institutionalise change which will break the grip of what has been referred to, in this paper, as the institutionalisation of inadequate and insecure housing and living conditions.

Notes

1 This article, while relating the experience of HIC, is a personal attempt to analyse the crisis in housing and land rights in the world today and a personal interpretation of the process through which the work has evolved. I do not claim, therefore, to represent the views of all my colleagues at HIC.

2 For a discussion of the reasoning behind this definition of the right to housing, see Miloon Kothari: *The Human Right to Adequate Housing: an inviolable right not only a social goal*, People's Decade for Human Rights Education, New York, January 1996. For the implications of such an overarching perspective on various aspects of people's processes and State action, see the HIC Declaration, 'Housing for All: Challenges for the world's governments', *HIC News,* Vol 2, No 2, May 1996.

3 These principles are based on the provisions contained in international human-rights law on the right to housing. For a discussion of these instruments and the texts of the articles, see the works cited in Note (2) above.

4 For more information about these campaigns and movements, contact the HIC-HRC or COHRE.

5 For the texts of international human-rights instruments on the right to housing, see UN Centre for Human Rights, *The Human Right to Adequate Housing*, Fact Sheet No. 21, United Nations, Geneva, 1995.

6 For a detailed consideration of the various dimensions of the 'national focus' programme and the advantages of such a programme, see: 'The Housing Rights Committee's National Focus Programme: A Discussion Note', HIC-HRC, Mexico, 1996.

7 For a survey of methods used by groups across the world, see COHRE, 'Campaigning for Housing Rights: Tested Strategies for Awareness and Mobilisation', Occasional Paper No. 6, Centre on Housing Rights and Evictions, Geneva and Mumbai (1997, forthcoming).

8 For a discussion of how the UN human-rights instruments system can be used at local and national levels, see COHRE, 'Sources #4: The Legal Struggle for Housing Rights: International and National Perspectives', COHRE, Netherlands, pp. 7–12, July 1994.

9 The Special Rapporteur's term, from 1992 to 1995, resulted in four reports. See in particular his final report: Centre for Human Rights, *The Right to Adequate Housing: Report of the Special Rapporteur*, Study Series no.7, World Campaign for Human Rights, New York and Geneva, 1996.

10 See in particular UN Commission on Human Rights resolution 1993/77. For the text of this and other UN instruments against forced evictions, see UN Centre for Human Rights, Forced Evictions, Fact Sheet no. 25, United Nations, 1996.

11 For the text of the Committee's General Comment, see op. cit. 5, pp. 39–47.

12 For a detailed survey of UN developments on forced evictions, see Miloon Kothari: 'The UN and forced eviction', *Development in Practice*, Volume 5, no. 1, February 1995, also reproduced in *Development in States of War* (edited by Deborah Eade, Oxford: Oxfam UK and Ireland, 1996).

13 For the texts of the main instruments of international human-rights law from which these principles are derived, see 'Human Rights: A Compilation of International Instruments', Volume 1 and Volume 2, United Nations, New York, 1995.

■ **Miloon Kothari** *was, until 1994, Joint Convenor of the Indian National Campaign for Housing Rights (NCHR), and was a founding member and Co-Director of the Centre on Housing Rights and Evictions (COHRE) from 1992 to 1997. Since 1991, he has represented Habitat International Coalition (HIC) at the UN Human Rights Bodies in Geneva. His book* Planned Segregation: Riots, Evictions and Dispossession in Jogeshwari East, Mumbai/Bombay, India, *written with Nasreen Contractor, was published in 1996 by COHRE and YUVA.*

This paper was first published in Development in Practice *Volume 7, Number 1, in 1997.*

■ *Information about Habitat International Coalition (HIC) is obtainable from its Mexico City headquarters: Cordobanes 24, Colonia San José Insurgentes, 03900 México DF, Mexico. Fax:+ (52 5) 593 5194. E-mail<hic@laneta.apc.org>*

Agrarian reform: a continuing imperative or an anachronism?

Cristina M. Liamzon

Introduction

In January 1994, Mexico was rudely awakened by a revolt which had been festering for decades in its southern State of Chiapas. On New Year's Day, indigenous people in the region joined in a rebellion to demand agrarian reform — something which was initiated in Mexico as a result of the 1910–1917 Revolution, but never reached Chiapas. The rebels' other demands concerned development, democracy, and respect: demands which have gone unmet for centuries (Cattanea, 1994).

Elsewhere in Latin America, Asia, and Africa, there are similar stories. Poor peasants working as small farmers, tenants, or landless workers become disenfranchised from the lands they till, which are taken over by landlords with minimal or no compensation, by banks to whom they are heavily indebted, or by big business or transnational corporations buying up land to expand their agri-business production. These farmers are left with little or nothing to sustain their livelihoods, as governments have abandoned agrarian reform in favour of less controversial rural programmes, and pursuit of a different development approach and model. Many such peasants end up as landless agricultural workers, selling their labour for below-subsistence wages, thus continuing the cycle of poverty and hunger.

Poverty, particularly in the rural areas, continues to increase. From 780 million considered poor in 1980, it is now estimated that over 800 million of the world's population are unable to feed themselves adequately. In Third World countries, a large proportion of poor people are rural. Although they are a heterogeneous population group, they share similar disabilities of limited assets, vulnerability to environmental factors, and inadequate access to basic health and educational services (FAO, 1986).

Yet it was little over 16 years ago when, in July 1979, 145 governments gathered in Rome to commit themselves to a Declaration and Programme of Action at the World Conference on Agrarian Reform and Rural Development (WCARRD). The UN Food and Agriculture Organisation (FAO) organised it with a view to alleviating rural poverty and adopting policies to achieve growth with equity and participation. Paragraph 8 of the Declaration states that 'sustained improvement of rural areas requires fuller and more equitable access to land, water and other natural resources; widespread sharing of economic and political power' (FAO, 1979). Agrarian reform was then deemed as to be the foundation of rural development and social and political stability. With land reform would follow the rural development which would stimulate the agricultural sector, leading the growth in gross domestic product. Shortly after, however, agrarian reform as a policy issue ceased to be emphasised, and has since virtually disappeared from the international development agenda. In recent global summits and conferences, land reform has not attracted the attention and interest of policy-makers. Since 1991, only two countries are considered still to be implementing agrarian reform within a wide-scale government focus: the Philippines and Zimbabwe (Melizcek, 1995), though South Africa is also now executing a major programme under Nelson Mandela's presidency.

This article discusses why it is that land reform has all but disappeared from the international development scene, and the reasons why agrarian reform must be brought back into the debate and adopted by governments as a continuing development policy for many countries. Agrarian reform continues to be a real need in many Third World countries, where persistent inequity is a serious impediment to the eradication of poverty and assurance of food security and rural livelihoods. The article goes on to illustrate an experience of agrarian reform in the Philippines, with a tripartite initiative by people's organisations (POs), non-governmental organisations (NGOs), and government, which is making some headway in advancing the country's agrarian-reform agenda. Many obstacles remain, however, to a thorough and successful implementation of the programme, presenting a challenge for POs, NGOs, and other reform advocates in the Philippines. The experience provides one example of how a concerted and committed effort, not just by government but by civil-society organisations operating within a legal and democratic framework, can realise some meaningful achievements in agrarian reform.

Defining land and agrarian reform

The term *land reform* has been used interchangeably with *agrarian reform* and continues to be so. Brown and Thiesenhusen (1983) define the former as 'the redistribution of ownership to achieve more equitable access to land and water', while the latter is 'land reform and supporting measures designed to make the reformed sector more productive'. *Agrarian reform* is thus used to refer to an integrated package of delivery systems. The distinction is highlighted by el Ghonemy (1989), who defines land reform as a 'strong demonstration of political commitment directed to abolish exploitation and attack rural poverty', while agrarian reform usually refers to 'land settlement schemes in public land, land registration, rent control, credit, etc'. He adds, however, that 'if there remains a skewed land distribution and rural power, there is no real land reform'.

Agrarian reform concerns the shifting of political and economic power from those who have traditionally enjoyed political and economic advantage, such as landlords, money-lenders, and traders, in favour of small farmers, tenants, and landless rural workers. This definition focuses on the primary importance of the redistributive component prior to other reforms. It is also in this context that the success of agrarian reforms must be evaluated.

Dwindling interest in agrarian reform

That land reform was on top of the development agenda up to the 1980s was evident with the holding of WCARRD in 1979 and the passage of the WCARRD Declaration and Programme of Action, more popularly known as the Peasants' Charter. In 1974, the World Bank claimed that redistributive land reform 'can go a long way towards solving the problem of rural poverty and without which it would be difficult to see much headway being made to reduce poverty in the rural areas' (World Bank, 1974:11). In the same year, the Bank's guidelines for lending to developing countries explicitly stated that 'in countries where increased productivity can effectively be achieved only subsequent to land reform, the Bank will not support projects which do not include land reform'.

The dwindling interest in pursuing agrarian reforms began in the mid-1980s, a consequence largely of what el Ghonemy calls a shift in the 'operational ideologies of major Western countries and international institutions'. The policies of Ronald Reagan as US President and of Margaret Thatcher as the British Prime Minister brought a radical move towards economic growth and support for market forces, especially large business interests, while also reducing government intervention, except in order to assist big business. The internal policies of the USA and the UK had a major influence on international institutions such as the World Bank, which these countries dominated. Support for such programmes as the redistribution of private land was quickly put on the sidelines. Instead, support was focused on liberalisation of trade, the promotion of export crops, and related policies. At the same time, faced with worsening problems of debt repayments, inflation, balance of payments deficits, and structural adjustment policies, many Third World governments became bankrupt, unable to meet fulfil their debt-servicing requirements or their social programmes for the poor. Third World countries were increasingly forced to veer away from rural development programmes that included agrarian reform, to those designed to expand the production of export crops to service external debts. This left little scope actively to pursue agrarian reform. As economic globalisation widens and deepens, the consolidation of lands by corporations, especially TNCs, for high-value export crops means that there is all the more reason for support for agrarian reform to weaken.

By 1987, various FAO studies showed deteriorating access to land for small farmers. Landlessness grew, there were large increases in very small land-ownership patterns, and large inequalities in sizes of land-holdings persisted.

Melizcek ascribes the disappearance of agrarian reform from the development agenda to the fact that there are only a few cases that could be claimed as successes. He cites the poor implementation of land-reform programmes, particularly for Central and Latin America, and the lack of political will and capacity of governments to carry out such reforms as the main causes for their failure. In countries like Brazil, Chile, Bangladesh, and Pakistan, only a small proportion of the surplus land was redistributed, and often it was of poor quality.

Rationale for agrarian reform

The main reason cited for implementing agrarian reform is that of social justice. Redistributive land reform and related measures redress possibly hundreds of years of unfair, often exploitative, social and productive relations between peasants and land-owners. With agrarian reform, tenants and landless workers may gain security of tenure on the lands that they, their parents, and forebears have tilled. Advocates of reform point to the need for governments to adjust property rights and to provide the necessary support services biased in favour of the rural poor. The issue of redistributive land reform is therefore, in the last analysis, a redistribution of political and economic power. Agrarian reform brings about a shift in political and economic power, and democratisation may take place.

Contrary to what many people believe, many land-holdings — particularly in the Third World—were not acquired through normal and regular market transactions. Rather, many studies have shown that political and institutional factors have been more prevalent in determining property rights. Consider, for example, the large land-holdings distributed by colonial administrations to loyal subjects in the former colonies; the lands taken by government fiat as a result of its affinity to and dependence on the support of landlords; the amassing of holdings largely through political connections. A Philippine study reveals the 'extraordinarily questionable nature of current landowners' claims to ownership of property' (Putzel, 1990). In addition, there are numerous examples of the way in which institutional factors such as government policies have continued to favour the interests of the better-off, providing the poor with minimal opportunities to improve their conditions. One need only note the long list of peasant upheavals over the years, as well as the more recent ones such as the Chiapas revolt, and the wholesale massacre of Guatemalan indigenous peoples and peasant populations throughout the 1970s and early 1980s.

But the argument of ethics and social justice, while appealing to social reformers, is certainly not the only basis for instituting agrarian reform. In very poor countries which have implemented it, there is much evidence to show that redistributive land reform and support services, implemented properly, have had a marked effect in alleviating poverty. As there is a close relation between poverty and landlessness in most rural communities, agrarian reform is fundamental to solving the problem. Land reform entails a redistribution of productive assets that would in turn result in a redistribution of income and an improvement in the living standards of the poor, particularly in terms of their food security, while not reducing aggregate output over the long term.

Farmers, who have long been victims of the powerlessness that results in a 'culture of silence', regain their sense of dignity and self-worth when they own the lands they till. The dependence and unequal social relations that historically existed between landlord and tenant are altered, and a better balance of social, economic, and political power likewise becomes possible, thereby strengthening the process of democratisation.

While there are examples of countries where land reform has failed, there are also many where agrarian reform has been successful and was a significant factor in the country's reduction of poverty, such as China, Laos, Vietnam, and Egypt. In some instances, agrarian reform was a significant ingredient in propelling the country's economic take-off, as in South Korea, Japan, and Taiwan. In these and other cases, government commitment and political will were crucial to the successful implementation of the reforms.

Experience in the Philippines

The Philippines is one of the very few countries worldwide where agrarian reform is still considered to be a major on-going government programme. For centuries, a high level of land concentration resulted in widespread peasant unrest. Peasants, with their dream of one day owning their land, became the nucleus of the Philippine revolt for independence beginning in 1896, and the nationalist struggle during World War II, which formed the base for the Communist Party and New People's Army. Peasant unrest pressured previous governments to institute certain reforms in the agrarian sector. Over the past 30 years, the legislature passed several laws aimed at redistributing land and ensuring security of tenure for tenant farmers. Among them were the Agricultural Land Reform Code of 1963 (Republic Act 3844), amended in 1971 by the Code of Agrarian Reforms, Republic Act 6389, and Presidential Decree (PD) 27 in October 1972, following the proclamation of Martial Law by former President Marcos. These laws and their implementation failed to respond adequately to the needs and demands of the peasants, thwarted by a lack of political will on the part of incumbent administrations, who were supported in this by the landed gentry. Poverty, found predominantly in the rural areas, intensified from the 1970s, and remains widespread.

After the 1986 revolution which ousted Marcos, NGOs and POs were hopeful that peasant demands for justice and a meaningful agrarian reform would finally be fulfilled. President Corazon Aquino, then eager to obtain peasant support, called her agrarian reform programme the centrepiece of her government. Wide consultations, known as NCARRD (Nationwide Consultations on Agrarian Reform and Rural Development), were organised soon after she came to power, involving peasant groups, NGOs, and academics, from local, municipal, sub-national, and national levels. What emerged was a set of policy recommendations that was submitted to top-level officials, to advise the government in its agrarian reform policy and implementation. Some twelve regional and national peasant federations, representing a wide spectrum of groups and ideologies, joined in a coalition called the Congress for a People's Agrarian Reform (CPAR). This peasant lobby formulated a People's Agrarian Reform Code (PARCODE), which they used as the basis for advocacy.

Contrary, however, to the hopes and clamour of the peasant sector and their partner NGOs, the much-awaited reform programme passed by the Philippine Legislature, the Comprehensive Agrarian Reform Law (CARL) (otherwise known as Republic Act 6657), turned out to be a much diluted version of the PARCODE.

Several peasant groups and their supporters, while expressing their perceptions of 'another betrayal', nevertheless assessed that there was an opportunity to use the CARL to encourage the implementation of the existing programme, while persisting in advocacy work to lobby for an improvement in the law. Thus, in 1989 the Philippine Partnership for the Development of Human Resources in Rural Areas (PhilDhrra) initiated the Tripartite Partnership of POs, NGOs, and government for Agrarian Reform and Rural Development (TriPARRD), in three pilot provinces in Antique, Bukidnon, and Camarines Sur (ABC), one in each of the country's three major island groupings. This experience of a tripartite partnership to facilitate agrarian reform in the Philippines offers one model of a collaborative, participatory mechanism that is showing encouraging results.

A partnership for agrarian reform

To install TriPARRD, PhilDhrra organised an extensive series of consultations between and among the POs, NGOs, and government agencies. POs and NGOs operating in each of the designated provinces held numerous discussions on the mechanics of collaborating, for the first time, on a large-scale project on the ground. They met with officials from the national through to the regional and local levels — officials whose support was seen as essential for the success in implementing the programme. This involved several key government agencies, such as the Department of Agrarian Reform (DAR); the Department of Environment and Natural Resources (DENR), which is responsible for public lands; the Department of Agriculture (DA), which is responsible for support services; and the Land Bank for financing. A technical advisory committee of NGO and PO representatives, together with several major university research institutions which helped to guide the programme implementation at each phase, was also set up at national level. This social infrastructure was a vital element in building the foundation for the programme's implementation. The three groups of actors—NGOs, POs, and government—institutionalised working relationships and partnerships to carry out a concerted, community-based agrarian reform, including joint training activities for government and NGO field workers. Initial suspicion generally evolved into positive collaboration, in pursuit of a more meaningful agrarian reform.

TriPARRD envisioned prototype activities in the three provinces to provide the necessary learning and experience that could be transferred as guidelines for other provinces. For the first phase, 28 sites were selected. The management realised that systematising the steps and processes for land titling and transfer of ownership was integral to the programme. As a result, several manuals have been produced to streamline these processes, as well as to guide successive phases in the areas covered.

For the initial stages, especially the consultative processes, programme structure, and mechanisms, and piloting in the three provinces, funds were provided by the US-based Ford Foundation, the Dutch NGO CEBEMO, and, subsequently, the Dutch government. By 1992, the programme had expanded to Quezon province, with the support of the German government, and in 1994 to Iloilo and Davao del Norte, with the support of the Dutch government. The TriPARRD Programme has served as a model for support for agrarian reform programmes from three major donor agencies — the European Union, the Belgian government, and the World Bank — and from 1995-96 is covering some 18 more provinces.

For TriPARRD, both the NGOs and POs are taking the lead, while the government, particularly under a current sympathetic leadership, has provided crucial support. In June 1993, the DAR launched its own 'tripartite strategy', following from TriPARRD's tripartism principle with its programme to develop a thousand Agrarian Reform Communities (ARCs).

Lessons for the future

TriPARRD, in its first six years, boasts of having facilitated the overall transfer of lands to farmer beneficiaries in over 60 per cent of the targeted land area in the pilot provinces. Over 50 small-scale projects aimed at improving the productive capacity and increasing the income levels of the new agrarian-reform beneficiaries are operating in each pilot area. A major objective of the TriPARRD Programme, to assist in the organising and/or strengthening of beneficiary groups, has led to the formation of over 30 POs in the 28 agrarian-reform communities, and also in provincial farmers' federations. This organisational growth is expected to enhance the capacity of the farmers to influence policy and to improve negotiations with government officials. TriPARRD has provided a model to deal with issues in the uplands and with tribal communities, which has led to the launching of TriPUD (Tripartite Partnership for Upland Development).

The TriPARRD Programme has, then, achieved a measure of success, to which many factors have contributed. A significant element has been the collaboration forged by the NGOs, together with their partner POs and four research institutions, to pursue a common programme, despite many limitations and hindrances. To some extent, the support and partnership with key government officials, particularly at the regional, provincial, and local levels, have been invaluable in moving the bureaucracy. Timely external support from several donors, who were willing to trust and invest in a process that had yet been untried, was very helpful in driving this forward at both national and local levels.

The programme is not without its problems, as a recent study of TriPARRD progress in one of the pilot provinces demonstrates: de los Reyes and Jopillo (1994) indicate that a primary weakness has been the insufficient organising work among the farmer beneficiaries to empower them to take full advantage of the benefits of agrarian reform and of their own continuous development. Organised farmers stand a stronger chance of getting the most out of the reform process. While NGOs generally claim community organisation and mobilisation as their comparative advantage over government, deficiencies in the organising and capacity-building of communities have been noted in several areas. This is partly explained by an insufficient number of well-trained organisers to work continuously with the beneficiary communities.

Another shortcoming was that only half of the land titles targeted, in this same province, were successfully transferred, despite the partnership between DAR and the NGOs. Community organisers had to steep themselves in the land-transfer process, and then train AR beneficiaries to go through the tedious process of doing the paper-work. The cumbersome bureaucratic requirements greatly delayed the process of transferring land titles, especially at the national level.

In part, NGOs lacked adequate knowledge of and grounding in both the process and the areas in which they were operating, which likewise delayed the land-transfer process. The frustrations of farmers and NGOs did, nevertheless, help to produce a manual to streamline the steps and recommend revised procedures by DAR.

TriPARRD has incorporated gender concerns, using community organising as its key strategy in seeking to introduce fair practices in beneficiary communities. But while there have been positive gains in raising awareness among PO members, much remains to be done. A 'Feminist Critique of the TriPARRD CO Technology', prepared by PhilDhrra (Matammu, 1996), noted that some of the gaps to be addressed include identifying women's felt needs, and activating the gender committees to become really responsive to them.

The tasks ahead

TriPARRD is presently operating in a political environment that favours the implementation of agrarian reform. However, a landlord-dominated Congress is ready to consider ways to resist extending such reform beyond its present mandate. The POs and NGOs are concerned that legislators with landed interests will influence other law-makers on the agrarian-reform process. A present loophole in CARL, which called for a ten-year phasing of the programme, has given landed interests the opportunity to set up counter-measures. The present government is intent on gaining the status of a newly industrialising country (NIC), following the path of its neighbours. This is causing a shift in priorities from equity-led considerations to those of the market. Already, there are ominous signs to indicate that agrarian reform is becoming a more limited, rather than more broad-based, programme in the country. Instead, agricultural efficiency along agri-business lines is being promoted as the country's major agricultural policy. The goal is to expand export production and increase efficiency, particularly in the agricultural sector. Small farmers and their holdings may not necessarily be seen as the most efficient way to expand commercial agriculture.

To date, the government has almost completed land transfers dating from the 1972 Marcos reform programme, covering rice and corn (maize) lands, as well as transfer of public lands. A more decisive test of government political will and capacity is in the programme's next phase: redistributing private landholdings of more than five hectares — which has been the most controversial section of the law. Continued financial, moral, and human resources are critically needed from government for acquisition of lands and the other support services, such as rural infra-structure, credit, extension, and markets, especially given the Ramos government's vision of the Philippines joining the next group of NICs in the region by the year 2000. Dwindling resources for land acquisition and other services will make it increasingly difficult for the DAR to implement the next phases of the programme, unless there is renewed political and financial support from the government, or from external or other sources.

Models of agrarian-reform programmes such as TriPARRD, while offering valuable lessons for mobilising PO/NGO efforts for facilitating the reform process, remain insufficient to determine the implementation of agrarian reform in the country. We include here the need to expand the base of peasants who, despite the obstacles, agree with the agrarian-reform programme and are committed to its implementation. This also implies the organisational consolidation of this peasant base, to strengthen their voice so that politicians and government officials will listen. The inability of the peasantry to speak in unity, and the divisions among them, constitute a major reason why the agrarian-reform programme is not taken seriously by law-makers. This is a major challenge for NGOs working in the rural areas, who need to strengthen their organising and mobilising skills to build up peasant groups.

Given the growing and increasingly strong opposition from landlords — allied with government officials and agri-business companies, including TNCs — a much more concerted endeavour is needed in support of agrarian reform among other sectors of civil society, beyond the work already being done by POs and NGOs. A way must be found to galvanise and mobilise groups involving media, academics, the church, even progressive business people and government officials, to be proactive in promoting the programme. To reach out to an uncommitted and unconcerned public and seek their support and backing is a long and difficult task. They need to be convinced that this is the only real path towards solving the centuries-old problem of peasant unrest and poverty in the rural areas of the Philippines. Without this, however, it will be difficult to defend the gains made over the past several years — which could spell doom for the continuation of a meaningful reform programme.

Many more arguments are presented to oppose agrarian reform, which its advocates must be able to counter. For example, opponents are quick to point out that agrarian reform is not only expensive, but that there is little assurance that farmers would be able to increase their productivity enough to supply their food requirements and those of the country. They claim that small farmers could not earn sufficient incomes from their land-holdings, an assertion that has already been disproved in several of the TriPARRD pilot areas. Farmer members of the Alamat Multipurpose Cooperative in the province of Camarines Sur, who became beneficiaries of agrarian reform with the help of TripARRD, have begun experimenting with diversifying crops and marketing their produce directly, moderately raising their incomes in the process.

There are concerns that land reform will cause fragmentation that will result in declining production, setting back the Philippines' progress towards NIC status. Officials in certain government agencies, big landowners, agri-business corporations, and business in general have expressed this fear, which is fuelling the movement to halt agrarian reform. Further debates centre on other more effective ways to address the issue of rural poverty than through redistribution, such as providing rural employment to assure regular incomes. It is often noted that, with popula-tion pressures, there are not enough lands to be distributed to all those in need, requiring an altogether different approach to reducing rural poverty. Another counter-argument cites the examples of farmers who, upon acquiring titles, immediately sell their parcels of land.

With opposition to agrarian reform gaining ground even among some progressives, ever more vigilance is needed on the part of POs, NGOs, and supporters of the reform process. In the words of one leading Philippine agrarian reform expert and advocate, Fr. Antonio Ledesma, SJ: 'Concerns over GATT and safety nets, sustainable development, and democratic participation all the more highlight the need for the speedy implementation and empowerment of small farmer communities.'

As Thiesenhusen asserts, 'the vision of the Philippines that it may soon become a "Tiger" overlooks the fact that at least South Korea and Taiwan had significant and egalitarian agrarian reforms prior to their robust industrialisation and initiation of rapid growth' (Thiesenhusen, 1990). Agrarian reform provides the foundation for achieving the agro-industrial base which the country needs, while at the same time ensuring local and national food security. It should be pursued within a framework of a sustainable rural development strategy, where farmers who have become owner-cultivators cultivate their lands intensively, in a diversified and sustainable way and within an agro-industrial setting. The pursuit of agrarian reform necessitates a shift in the government's present priorities, which favour the kind of economic growth that is not premised on equity, environmental protection, and building of local self-reliance. These are but some of the issues that the advocates of agrarian reform must collectively address to counter opposition to it, and without which reform cannot advance.

The future of agrarian reform in other countries

Peasant groups and their support NGOs in many Third World countries continue to call for redistributive land reform or agrarian reform, since this is no longer given the priority it deserves within development policy, having been sidelined by a marked move in the 1980s to seek economic growth and liberalisation at all costs, at the expense of majority of the countries and poor peoples in the South. At the NGO Global Forum on Food Security during FAO's Fiftieth Anniversary Celebration held in October 1995 in Quebec, POs and NGOs, particularly from the Third World, unequivocally stated the need for a renewed effort to bring agrarian reform back to the fore of the international development agenda.

The November 1996 FAO World Food Summit — taking place as this issue is published — presents an opportunity to underscore the importance of ensuring food security, through agrarian reform, for rural households and other vulnerable sectors in the rural areas. When small producers know that the land they till is theirs, they will be motivated to invest in it in order to improve agricultural productivity.

From WCARRD to the World Food Summit, the world must be reminded that if hunger, poverty, and malnutrition in the Third World are to be effectively addressed, technological fixes such as the Green Revolution are not the answer, unless linked to socio-political and economic solutions. Equity issues such as redistributive land reform and other agrarian reforms are policy imperatives which must continue to be actively pursued.

References

Brown, M. and W. Thiesenhusen (1983) FAO LR Nos. 1 and 2, Rome

Cattanea, A. T. (1994) 'Raining stove: Chiapas rebels fight for agrarian reform', FAO CERES 148, July-August 1994, Rome

FAO (1979) *WCARRD Declaration*, Rome.

el Ghonemy, M. R. (1989) *The Political Economy of Rural Poverty — The Case for Land Reform*, London and New York: Routledge

Matammu, L. (1996) 'Feminist Critique of PhilDhrra's TriPARRD Community Organising Technology', (1996), Manila: PhilDhrra

Melizcek, H. (1995) 'If poverty is the problem, land reform must be part of the answer', FAO CERES 152, March-April 1995, Rome

PhilDhrra (1991) *Manual for TriPARRD Implementors,* Vol.1, Manila

Putzel, J. (1990) 'Why it mattered little who was in charge', *Lupa at Buhay — Agrarian Reform in the Philippines,* Amsterdam: PhilDev

de los Reyes, R. and S. Jopillo (1994) *Waging Agrarian Reform*, Manila: IPC

Thiesenhusen, W. (1990) 'Recent progress toward agrarian reform in the Philippines', *International Issues in Agrarian Reform: Past Experiences, Future Prospects,* Report of the Colloquium on Agrarian Reform, 26–30 March 1990, QuezonCity

■ **Cristina Liamzon** *is a Fellow of the People-Centered Development Forum, and responsible for its Rome Resource Centre. She was involved in the initial stages of the TriPARRD Programme as former National Coordinator of PhilDhrra. She is the permanent Representative of the Asian NGO Coalition for Agrarian Reform and Rural Development (ANGOC) to FAO.*

This paper was first published in Development in Practice *Volume 6, Number 4, in 1996.*

The ethics of immigration controls: issues for development NGOs[1]

Andy Storey

Introduction

Asylum and refugee movements have become matters of enormous interest recently in the media and among policy-makers in Europe. They have also generated considerable comment by development NGOs, usually supportive of the interests of refugees and asylum applicants. For example, NGOs have pointed out that, while European governments and much of the European media focus on the allegedly overwhelming numbers of asylum-seekers seeking sanctuary in Europe, 83 per cent of the world's refugees live in 'Third World' countries, many of which play host to proportionately far more people than do the countries of Western Europe, and with far fewer resources.[2]

That the rights of asylum-seekers in Europe need to be defended more vigorously than at present would probably be accepted by almost all development NGOs, and by a sizeable minority of the general public. But there is an even more fundamental issue which has received very little attention to date. This concerns whether development NGOs should question the ethics of global immigration controls in general, and not just the barriers to the movement of those fleeing from persecution.

Could it not be argued that immigration restrictions constitute a form of 'global apartheid', ensuring that poorer sections of world society are prevented, by legal and physical force, from sharing in total world riches?[3] This paper seeks to develop this theme, by arguing that immigration controls are based on dubious ethical and practical foundations, and that NGOs should be more willing than hitherto to challenge their validity. The paper is deliberately polemical, seeking to counter some widely accepted views on the subject. Substantial reference is made to the writings of Susan

George, both because she presents a good summary of much of the 'conventional wisdom' on this issue, and also because the well-deserved respect which her views command within the development community means that her arguments may carry some weight among development NGOs.

The immigration 'boomerang'

In her most recent book on the debt crisis — *The Debt Boomerang: How Third World Debt Harms Us All*[4] — Susan George discusses its cost for the 'First World' through the impact of 'boomerangs' like lost market opportunities and global environmental destruction. One chapter — 'The fifth boomerang: immigration' — argues that the 'First World' will, to a certain extent, also pay a price for continued debt and under-development in the 'Third World' in the form of influxes of poor, would-be immigrants seeking to escape poverty in their own countries.

While George is surely correct in her identification of this 'boomerang' effect, my central problem with her approach to the immigration issue relates to the very legitimacy of immigration control. Her views are encapsulated in her statement that:

> The right-wing, knee-jerk 'we shall fight them on the beaches' riposte is as inappropriate as the 'liberal' or 'progressive' notion that the rich countries can somehow maintain open borders.[5]

The notion that the rich countries cannot (and should not) allow free entry to anyone and everyone would probably be accepted by many commentators. In June 1991, British Prime Minister John Major remarked that 'we must not be wide open to all-comers just because Rome, Paris and London are more attractive than Bombay or Algiers'.[6] Most lobbying on this issue by human-rights groups focuses on the need to afford protection to 'genuine' asylum-seekers, who should be let in, as opposed to 'economic migrants', who simply want a better life and who, according to many, should be excluded.

I am not suggesting that lobbying for the rights of asylum-seekers is not a necessary and practical activity (the concluding section of this article returns to this topic). My point is that it can legitimately be argued that everyone in the South has a right to a better life, and the North has no right to deny access to it, wherever it may be found.

Many would accept that, in an ideal world, everyone should have the freedom to move to, and live and work in, any part of the globe. Such freedom would enhance the range of choices open to any individual. Unless it can be clearly demonstrated that there is a good reason why that freedom is undesirable, then it can plausibly be suggested that there should be an *a priori* presumption in favour of it. This position, of course, rests upon a strong (and openly idealist) assumption. Others may disagree with it, and thus reject the substance of my argument. But such disagreement would at least bring differences in underlying value judgements to the fore. At present, most objections to freedom of movement are assumed to be so self-evidently valid that the values on which they rest are never seriously examined. I will now look at four of the most common such objections.

The arguments against unlimited immigration

The 'decent living' argument

When former French premier Michel Rocard said: 'We can't take in the whole of the world's misery', he was, according to Susan George, 'speaking the literal truth'.[7] But why could not the North take in anyone from the South who wanted to move there? Susan George argues that further immigration would make it difficult to 'ensure a decent living ... for those immigrants who are already in the North'. But how does one define a 'decent living'? Average GNP *per capita* is US$80 in Mozambique, compared with US$17,820 in France (though immigrants, of course, usually earn much less). If people in Mozambique are expected to live (or die) on such a small sum, then the argument that France could not ensure a 'decent living' (by the standards of the poorest countries of the world) for a greatly increased population starts to look a little threadbare.

One long-term consequence of totally free population movement would be to ensure greater equality of incomes around the world: high-income locations would attract in-flows, pushing down incomes; and low-income locations would suffer out-flows, raising average incomes for those left behind. If total world income were evenly distributed, each person would receive somewhere in the region of US$4,000, which would represent a major drop in French living standards, but would be sufficient to ensure that no-one in the world died of starvation. In other words, it would mean the fulfilment for all of the minimal conditions for a 'decent living'. Undermining the present income levels of all those living in the North (immigrants and indigenous) can therefore be seen as being in the interests of broader global justice.

It might be argued that unrestrained in-flows of immigrants would not equalise incomes within countries: the immigrants would remain at the bottom end of the Northern labour market, in worsening conditions of unemployment and poverty. There are two responses to this: first, unemployment and poverty in the North may still be preferable to their equivalents in the South; second, the correct response to relative poverty in the North is surely to press for greater equality and justice *within* Northern societies, not to help to sustain injustice at a global level by keeping the numbers of the poor in the North down to 'manageable' proportions.[8] Susan George bemoans the fate of those immigrants 'living physically and socially unprotected lives on the margins of American society'.[9] But that deplorable situation calls for increased protection and de-marginalisation, not barriers to movement.

The vision of a world with an equal distribution of income between and within countries is, of course, utopian; but it highlights the fact that those who argue that immigration undermines the possibility of a 'decent living' for all do so from a standpoint of relative affluence. One does not have to believe that greater global equality is a good thing in itself. The point is simply that, if such equality arises as a side-effect of the exercise of freedom of movement, then it cannot be condemned simply because it depresses the incomes of a certain group of relatively well-off people. From a global perspective, there is no convincing argument against freedom of movement on these grounds.

Practical evidence also rebuts the suggestion that immigration would make it impossible to provide a 'decent living' for all in the recipient countries. By far the heaviest relative concentrations of immigrants or refugees are to be found in some of the poorest countries of the world. For example, in 1987, Malawi, with an average *per capita* income of US$180 was hosting at least 200,000 Mozambican refugees, equivalent to 2.4 per cent of its population. Pakistan with an average *per capita* income of $370 played host to 3 million Afghan refugees, equivalent to 2.7 per cent of its population.[10] Perhaps if these poor countries had the means to prevent such in-flows, they would do so. But this is beside the point; what is crucial is that they *do* absorb the new arrivals. If countries which are much poorer than those of the North can carry such 'burdens', then the argument that rich countries cannot offer at least equivalent hospitality is shown to be patently spurious.

The 'relative freedom from racism' argument

Susan George argues that further immigration to France and elsewhere would make it difficult, if not impossible, to ensure 'relative freedom from racism'[11] for those immigrants already in the North, thus implicitly accepting the case for differential immigration control between blacks and whites.

Racism against immigrants is, of course, a problem which needs to be tackled — but it is not a problem which legitimises immigration barriers, any more than discrimination against gay and lesbian people legitimises policies which encourage (or force) people not to declare their sexuality. To accept immigration controls is to accept defeat in the struggle against racism. Just as poor living and working conditions for immigrants constitute arguments for the elimination of the conditions, rather than the people, so racist attacks constitute arguments for the elimination of racism, rather than its victims.

Implicit in Susan George's argument is the notion that uncontrolled (non-white) immigration would generate uncontrollable racist reactions, leading to situations of extreme crisis. She cites a study from the early 1980s which predicts that Los Angeles could well 'become 75 per cent Hispanic in the year 2000 with unemployment rates quite possibly as high as 12 to 15 per cent. Such hardships would then make Hispanics the most easily targeted scapegoats for the economic grievances of "indigenous workers".'[12] This scenario is surely an argument in favour of immigration: the more 'Hispanics' there are, the less chance there is that they can be easily persecuted. When a grouping constitutes 75 per cent of the population, it is in a far stronger position to resist racism than if it constitutes a vulnerable minority. However, immigration controls institutionalise the present vulnerable positions of minorities.

Damaging the economies of the poor countries

The out-flow of people from poor countries which the lifting of immigration restrictions might encourage would, it is argued, lower the development potential of those countries, since their most valuable resource, the most energetic and intelligent sections of the population, would apply their abilities elsewhere.

There is some truth in this argument, but it hardly constitutes a justification for the maintenance of immigration controls on the part of the North. If such controls were to be rationalised on this basis, it would amount to the North saying, 'It would be better for you if you stayed where you are. We are enforcing these controls for your own good.' Such a patronising attitude would not be accepted as legitimate by development NGOs in other areas of North/South relations, including trade issues:

Developing countries may well decide to limit their involvement in international trade; that is their right. What is not acceptable is that the developed countries should, unilaterally, make this decision for them.[13]

Similarly, people in developing countries may choose not to migrate, or their governments may seek to persuade them not to do so; that is their right. Northern governments have no right to make those choices for them.

While the right of Northern governments to restrict Southern emigrant flows can be rejected, Southern societies do undoubtedly suffer through out-flows of labour, especially of skilled labour. The 1992 *Human Development Report* from the United Nations Development Programme (UNDP)[14] provides some striking examples:

- The Philippines lost 12 per cent of its qualified professionals to the USA in the 1970s.
- By 1987, nearly one-third of Africa's skilled professionals had moved to Europe.
- Sudan lost 30 per cent of its engineers and 45 per cent of its surveyors in 1978 alone.
- In Ghana, 60 per cent of the doctors who trained there in the early 1980s have now emigrated.

A US study estimated that in 1971-72, the South as a whole lost an 'investment' of US$20,000 for each skilled emigrant, amounting to a total loss of US$646 million. Only some of these losses are recouped through remittances.

The current immigration policies of Northern countries serve to encourage this 'brain drain', by selectively allowing entry to some highly skilled and qualified people from the South:

> The industrial countries, in what is effectively a 'buyers' market' for migrants, have been setting higher and higher levels of qualification —giving preference to highly skilled workers, or to those who bring capital with them, or letting in only political refugees ...
>
> The industrial countries are now in a position to ask not just for labour but also for money. Canada and the United States, for example, have been giving preference to investors and are said to have attracted millions of dollars in this way.[15]

There is a socio-economic cost associated with emigration from Southern countries. And, of course, there is more to emigration than a narrow calculation of economic benefits and losses; the social and psychological impacts should be accorded equal importance. These are not invariably negative, but it is true that emigration imposes huge costs on those who move and on those who are left behind. A practical illustration of this occurs when males migrate from rural households, leaving women with increased responsibilities and workloads, as well as emotional burdens, often in situations of great economic hardship.

Would it make sense for Southern societies to suffer increased out-migration when the socio-economic losses associated with present emigration levels are so significant? Are the potential social losses sufficiently severe to justify, in the interests of the overall good, limitations on individuals' rights to move? While the implementation of such restrictions on the part of Northern governments might be cynical and indefensible in principle, could the restrictions be exempted from criticism by development NGOs on the grounds that their ultimate (unintended) impact was to limit damage to Southern economies and societies?

I think the answer to these questions is 'no'. For a start, emigration confers economic benefits, as well as losses, on sending societies. In 1989, Southern countries obtained approximately US$25 billion in official remittances from workers in Northern and Gulf countries; in the 1980-85 period, such remittances covered around 20 per cent of the merchandise import bill in Turkey and Morocco, while the figure was even higher for Jordan, Pakistan, and Sudan in 1989.[16] These figures refer only to official remittances — many emigrant workers send money home through unofficial and unrecorded channels. These remittances stimulate knock-on economic activity in the emigrant-sending country; the 'multiplier effect' of emigrants' remittances has been estimated at 2.2 in Egypt and 2.4 in Pakistan: i.e., US$1 of remittances ultimately boosts national income by US$2.2–2.4.[17]

At present, immigration restrictions enormously limit the potential economic benefits of remittances. The UNDP has calculated the cost of immigration restrictions to developing countries:

> Developing countries already have extensive unemployment and underemployment, combined with population growth of 2.2% a year. And workers who migrate could expect much higher salaries overseas. So, to suggest that, say, 2% of the labour force in the developing world would choose to move each year if there were no restrictions is a cautious estimate indeed. If such workers earned no more than a poverty-line salary in industrial countries (around $5,000 a year), they would earn $220 billion a year. Of this, between $40 and $50 billion would be sent home as remittances.

The benefit of remittances would be cumulative at first as more people found a place in richer societies, but would then level off as immigrants started to sever close links with their home country. Over five years, however, they might reach $200 billion a year. This income would have an even greater impact on GNP (possibly double) through the multiplier effect mentioned earlier. Offset against all this income would have to be reduced growth opportunities because of the loss of skilled workers. Even using very conservative assumptions, immigration controls deny developing countries income (direct and indirect) of at least $250 billion a year.[18]

A significant factor in the UNDP scenario is that it involves a loss of only 2 per cent of the Southern labour force: if emigration were limited to such relatively low levels, then its negative social repercussions would be much smaller than those already incurred by European countries such as Ireland and Portugal.

Further, emigration on an even larger scale may make particular sense in situations of extreme poverty, unemployment, and population growth — conditions which characterise much of the South:

Some 38 million extra people join the labour force [in the South] each year. Added to the more than 700 million people already unemployed or underemployed [40 per cent of the labour force], this means that one billion new jobs must be created, or improved, by the end of the decade — equivalent to the total population of the North.[19]

In this context, emigration may be the only means to relieve intolerable pressures. Given previous experience in the North, out-migration may be a vital element in a particular stage of the development process, a notion which Northern governments now conveniently ignore:

Eurocentrism has quite simply ignored the fact that the demographic explosion of Europe, caused, like the analogous explosion in the Third World, by capitalist transformation, was accompanied by massive emigration to the Americas and a few other regions of the world. Without this massive emigration, Europe would have had to undertake its agricultural and industrial revolutions in conditions of demographic pressure analogous to those in the Third World today. The number of people of European ancestry living outside of Europe is currently twice the size of the population of the migrants' countries of origin.[20]

Development NGOs do not have to endorse a specifically capitalist transformation in the South to discern the relevant historical parallel: without some outlet for 'surplus' labour, it may be impossible for regions to transform their socio-economic systems.

Of course, it would be ideal if no-one were to become 'surplus' to a system, and if equitable global development could provide everyone with the opportunity of making a decent living in their home region. Pursuing such objectives — through calls for increased and improved development aid, fairer terms of trade, debt relief, and other such activities — is valuable, because it helps to expand people's choices and alleviate the pressures which might otherwise make emigration or destitution the only available alternatives. But calls for measures to stimulate development in poor regions should be justified on their own merits: the alleviation of poverty and the expansion of choice. These are independent of the case for the free movement of people, which also stands in its own right.[21]

The various economic arguments which can be made for the free movement of people — for instance, that it may permit certain types of socio-economic transformation — are not justifications in themselves for free movement. Their importance lies in their being counterweights to the contention that migration will necessarily damage the economies of poor societies. While there are arguments on both sides, there would seem to be no clear basis for preventing migration in order to protect the interests of society as a whole. In other words, if one starts (as I do) from the presumption that people should have the freedom to move, then only firm evidence that the exercise of such freedom would actively damage the welfare of society as a whole can be used to justify limiting it.

An argument which mirrors the suggestion that free movement of people would damage the economies of poor countries is that free movement facilitates the perpetuation of unjust social structures. In other words, by 'draining off' the unemployed and the otherwise dissatisfied, migration relieves social tensions which would otherwise have led to irresistible pressure for the radical reform of society. There may be some truth in this. It may also be true that the absence of emigration merely contributes to unemployment and poverty, in turn generating apathy and disillusion: inertia, rather than revolutionary fervour, characterises many impoverished societies. Equally, if social pressure was brought to a head by the lack of the emigration 'safety-valve', it could very well be channelled into reactionary forms, such as the revival of fundamentalism or fascism. These two considerations — that the lack of emigration outlets might not generate much pressure for change, and that if such change was generated it might not be positive — strongly suggest that people's freedom to move should not be overruled on the basis of a tentative hope that this will cause progressive social change.

Accepting a 'free market' ideology

Samir Amin has highlighted the hypocrisy of Northern governments' attitudes to the immigration issue:

> The litany of the market cure, invoked at every turn, comes to a dead halt here: to suggest that in a henceforth unified world, human beings, like commodities and capital, should be at home everywhere is quite simply unacceptable. The most fanatical partisans of the free market suddenly find at this point an argument for the protectionism that they fustigate [sic] elsewhere as a matter of principle.[22]

Amin's point is amusing and perceptive. The hypocrisies of Northern governments, by turns encouraging and repelling migration from the South, depending on the needs of their industries, are not confined to this aspect of the issue. But the implication that in a world of increasingly free movement of goods, services, and capital, people (labour) should also be free to move, begs the question, 'Is this the kind of world development that NGOs want?'[23] Many 'alternative' or 'progressive' commentators reject the argument that the world must increasingly accept, as ends in themselves, completely free trade and free movement of the factors of production. They would argue instead for the increased exercise of democratic control over capital and trade. It may be feared that to promote the free movement of people would appear to endorse the free-trade and free-markets paradigm, and thus reinforce a model of development which renders it increasingly difficult for people to determine their own development priorities.

There is certainly a logic to opposing development which elevates the free movement of the inanimate (but not the animate) to the level of sacred dogma. But an appropriate alternative need not accept the free movement of people and things, nor the need to restrict the movement of both. At present, things (capital, commodities) are free to move, but people are not; development NGOs can plausibly argue for the opposite. In order that people can democratically design and implement their own development agendas — at local, regional, and global levels — controls on the movement of goods may sometimes be necessary. If so, there is every reason to support such controls. But people should not be treated in the same manner: if people wish to move, they must be allowed to do so. Even if such movement might have negative effects on others (and this is debatable), one of the core values of a truly 'alternative' development strategy to be propounded by NGOs should surely be the maximisation of human freedom.

Before the fall of the Berlin Wall, there was a joke which ran as follows:

> **East German politician:** 'What makes East Germany different from West Germany is that we care about our people, while you care about your money.' **West German politician:** 'Yes—that's why we lock up our money and you lock up your people.'

The joke, insofar as it suggested that the West German government did not treat people like objects, was inaccurate: West Germany did not lock up many of its people, but it was quite prepared to lock out those it did not want. However, the distinction which the joke highlights between restrictions on money and people is one which proponents of a people-centred development approach could usefully adopt.

Conclusion

Alternative value judgements

This paper aims to demonstrate that if one starts from a certain value judgement — in this case, a presumption that freedom of movement should be maximised on the grounds of broadening the range of human choices — then this casts serious doubts on the objections commonly raised to the idea of unlimited South—North migration.

The arguments for freeing up such migration could have been made on alternative grounds: for example, that the capitalist system has historically exploited Southern labour, attracting some of it to the North to perform menial jobs (where illegality and racism serve the useful function of limiting workers' rights, and the fight for those rights); but keeping most of it in the countries of the South, where it can be exploited by Northern transnational companies and others. If this position were to be adopted, the argument against immigration controls could be formulated in terms of resistance to imperialism and to its historical (as well as on-going) exploitation of Southern labour. This is the position articulated in the writings of, among others, A. Sivanandan.[24]

Whatever position is adopted, reasoned argument demands that the underlying values and/or analytical frameworks be made explicit, whether they are the 'liberal' notion of increasing individual choice or the 'socialist' conception of the injustice of class oppression. Unfortunately, the debate to date has often been based on sloppy assumptions rooted in supposed 'common sense'. This article has sought to challenge some of these assumptions.

Questions of tactics

Reference has been made already to the distinction which many human-rights groups draw between asylum-seekers, who are fleeing persecution (and who are entitled under international law to protection in exile); and 'economic migrants', who are 'merely' trying to improve their lifestyles. The thrust of this paper has been that all such 'economic migrants' should also be allowed access to the North. However, it can be convincingly argued that if human-rights groups adopted such a position, governments would dismiss it and use the excuse to tighten restrictions against all-comers.

This raises questions of tactics: in a situation where the best that can be achieved is the protection of a relatively small number of people (asylum-seekers) who are in conditions of dire insecurity, then it is appropriate to concentrate on attempts to safeguard their welfare. For instance, many people are concerned with promoting greater equality between everyone in society, but this does not mean that they will not prioritise a campaign to protect the living standards of those at the lowest income levels, such as those depending on social-welfare payments.

Challenges — to ourselves and to the State

While recognising tactical imperatives, the philosophical premise of this paper could nevertheless be adopted as part of a broader (and longer-term) alternative conception of the 'world order' by development NGOs and others. The implications for us are enormous: are we prepared to accept sharing 'our' wealth and 'our' space with those poorer than ourselves? Accepting free movement poses far more direct challenges to our standards of living than, for example, massively increased development aid. It therefore challenges in a much more profound way the depth of our commitment as development NGOs to an equitable distribution of global resources.

To repeat an earlier point, this is not to suggest that development NGOs should abandon efforts to, for example, ease rural–urban migration (often a precursor to international migration) by promoting development in rural Southern areas. Such efforts remain justified on their own merits: they allow people to make a real choice between staying in rural areas and migrating. The question here is how we should respond to that choice, once it is made, in favour of migration.

Accepting free movement forces us to examine our conceptions of the nation state and its role: 'There is a strong desire among the public and politicians in the industrial democracies to control migration, for what seems to be a simple reason. The control of borders (territorial closure) is the essence of state sovereignty.'[25]

Development NGOs should ask themselves why they should be willing to accept the logic of State-based analyses:

> No issue today so sharply differentiates internationalists and national reformists as that of the international migration of workers. The issue at stake is a challenge to the very existence of the national State and its prerogatives in the control of a territory and the inhabitants. Much of the politics of the Left is concerned with gaining control of the State. Deploring the ill treatment of immigrants is seen, not as an attack on the powers of the State, but as an argument for ending all immigration... Accepting the right of the State to control immigration is accepting its right to exist, the right of the ruling class to exist as a ruling class, the right to exploit, the 'right' to a world of barbarism.[26]

It is time that development NGOs took this challenge more seriously.

Notes

1 Thanks to Deborah Eade and to an independent referee for valuable comments on an earlier draft. The usual disclaimer applies.

2 Figures are from S. Egan and A. Storey (1992), 'European asylum policy: a fortress under construction', *Trocaire Development Review 1992*, p. 51.

3 I am indebted to Teresa Shortall for this analogy.

4 Susan George (1992), *The Debt Boomerang: How Third World Debt Harms Us All*, London: Pluto Press in association with the Transnational Institute.

5 Ibid, p. 112.

6 Quoted in the *Observer* newspaper, 30 June 1991.

7 George (1992), p. 112.

8 There are parallels here with the argument that poverty within the South should be tackled primarily by population control, an argument which Susan George has consistently rejected in her previous writings.

9 George (1992), p. 115.

10 Figures on refugee numbers in Malawi are from F. Cuny and B. Stein (1990), 'Prospects for and promotion of spontaneous repatriation', in G. Loescher and L. Monahan (eds.), *Refugees and International Relations*, Oxford: Clarendon Press, p. 300. The figures on refugees in Pakistan are from the introduction by Loescher to the same book on page 14. Comparative population data are drawn from the World Bank's 1991 *World Development Report*. In the summer of 1992, Yemen accepted at least 50,000 refugees from Somalia; a diplomat there commented: 'It's amazing really. Yemen has nothing and yet they still have let these people in, and have received hardly any credit for it from the international community ...' (Guardian, 9 July 1992).

11 George (1992), p. 112.

12 Ibid, p. 115.

13 A. Matthews (1991), *EC Trade Policy and the Third World: an Irish Perspective*, Dublin: Trocaire and Gill and Macmillan, p. 6.

14 New York: Oxford University Press, p. 57.

15 Ibid, pp. 55–6.

16 Ibid, p. 56.

17 Ibid, p. 57.

18 Ibid, p. 58.

19 Ibid, p. 54.

20 S. Amin (1988), *Eurocentrism*, London: Zed Books, p. 112.

21 A relatively minor point is that the scale of losses which the South incurs through immigration restrictions (estimated by the UNDP at US$250 billion a year) could hardly be 'compensated for' without massively increased resource transfers. For example, if the UN's development aid target of 0.7 per cent of GNP was to be met by the Northern countries, then this would involve increased aid to the South of less than $60 billion per year, less than one-quarter of the estimated losses incurred through immigration barriers. Debt relief and trade reform would generate additional resource transfers, but, given that these are things which should occur in any event in the interests of global justice, it is hardly appropriate to suggest that they be used as 'compensations' for the maintenance of unjust restrictions on the freedom of movement.

22 Amin (1988), pp. 112–13.

23 To be fair, this is probably not what Amin was actually implying; he was more likely using the contrast as an illustration of double standards.

24 See, for example, A. Sivanandan (1990), 'Racism 1992', in his Communities of Resistance: writings on black struggles for socialism, London/New York: Verso, pp. 153–60.

25 J. F. Hollifield (1992), *Immigrants, Markets and States: the political economy of postwar Europe*, Cambridge/London: Harvard University Press, p. 5.

26 N. Harris (1991), *City, Class and Trade: Social and Economic Change in the Third World*, London/New York: Tauris, p. 152.

■ **Andy Storey** *is a lecturer at the Development Studies Centre, Kimmage Manor, Dublin. Besides refugee and immigration issues, his current research interests include ethnicity and processes of State formation.*

This paper was first published in Development in Practice *Volume 4, Number 3, in 1994.*

The right to protection from sexual assault: the Indian anti-rape campaign

Geetanjali Gangoli

Introduction

Rape and child sexual abuse (CSA) are among the most discussed yet 'unknown' parts of Indian social and legal life. The Indian Women's Movement (IWM) focused on an extensive campaign on rape, culminating in a legal amendment in 1983. As someone who is within the IWM, yet not uncritical of it, I look here at some of the dilemmas. They relate to the realities of rape victims, to debates within the IWM, and to the legal structure. The following account may be fragmented and incomplete, but is not, I hope, unrepresentative. I contend that the discourse concerning rape is one about women's sexuality, in the legal arena, in Indian feminist practice, and in the areas of overlap between them. I trace the history of the IWM campaign, then examine the language of the law and certain case judgements, and finally explore the current debate and stands within the IWM on the issue.

The anti-rape campaign

The 1980 anti-rape campaign began in protest at a Supreme Court judgement which acquitted two policemen charged with raping and molesting a tribal girl, Mathura, in a police station in Maharashtra. In 1979, four law professors at Delhi University had written an open letter to the Chief Justice, protesting against the judgement, saying that it 'snuffs out all aspiration for the protection of human rights of millions of Mathuras'.

Mathura, aged 16 years, was orphaned in childhood. She was brought to the police station by her brother, alleging that she had eloped with her lover. As she was about to leave, the policemen detained her. She was then raped by Ganpat (one of the accused), while Tukaram watched. Mathura's case was registered by the police only because of the pressure exerted by an angry crowd outside the station. The sessions court acquitted the rapist, stating that 'there was no satisfactory evidence to prove that Mathura was below 16 years ... [She] is a shocking liar whose testimony is riddled with falsehood and improbabilities'. The judge held that while sexual intercourse between Ganpat and Mathura had taken place, there is 'a world of difference between sexual intercourse and rape'.

The Bombay High Court later overturned the judgement and convicted both defendants, who later appealed and had their conviction set aside. The court held that, since she had not raised any alarm, Mathura's allegations of rape were untrue. Besides, since Mathura 'was habituated to sexual intercourse', she could not be 'so overpowered by fear that she could not resist'.[1]

The professors' open letter prompted a nationwide campaign. In Bombay, the Forum Against Rape (FAR) was formed in 1980, mainly by left-of-centre women. It was '... an ad-hoc body ... westernised, with cosmopolitan values, well informed about the western liberation movement'.[2] But the FAR was not alone. Independent women's groups emerged, such as Stree Sangharsh and Saheli in Delhi, and Vimochana in Bangalore. The anti-rape campaign took different, but complementary, forms: firstly, it aimed to mobilise public support, through songs, skits and plays; and secondly to lobby the State to review and reform the law on rape. Both were in some senses revolutionary: in conservative Indian society, the taboo on speaking the word 'rape' was broken — in public, and by women. The shock value of women marching on the streets singing songs and shouting slogans about rape made people sit up and take notice.[3]

> *Uncle, was it you who felt desire,*
> *Took her body with your gold-ringed hand?*
> *We are not just female servants, sister,*
> *And I am damned if I'll just die.*
> *Joined together there is power-sister*
> *No-one hears the victim's sigh.*
> (Delhi street song[4])

The fledgling IWM succeeded to an extent in its 'material' aims: the country-wide debate forced the State to initiate changes in the rape law, leading to the 1983 amendment. While this is among the movement's more tangible 'successes', here I focus on other aspects of the anti-rape campaign, many of which remain unresolved.

The 1980s campaign focused almost exclusively on custodial rape: the rape of remand prisoners or innocent women by police and other 'custodians' of law and order. This was not the first protest in the country, against the use of rape by the State to suppress democratic movements of tribals, peasants, workers, and political dissidents. But it was only in the 1980s that it emerged as not only a civil-rights issue, but as a women's issue. IWM activists suggest that the new movement could rally around the anti-rape issue so effectively because the excesses of the 1975 emergency declared by the Indira Gandhi government had by that time removed the last vestiges of faith in the State — at least for the middle classes, who had still nurtured some belief in the benevolent and progressive nature of the Indian State since 1947: '[during] the emergency ... it was the first time that middle class women saw the oppressive machinery of the state in action'.[5]

The focus on custodial rape was significant, for it directly challenged the excesses and the brutality of State patriarchy. But somewhere along the way, an aspect of the Mathura case was lost: she was only 16 years old at the time of the rape, a legal minor. And, as some within the IWM have felt in moments of introspection, Mathura herself was lost. She was oblivious of the fact that her case had made history. In her own social context, she was isolated. The police were also harassing her as a woman of loose character. Years later, on hearing of what had later happened to Mathura, one of the law professors who had written the open letter was to write:

> ... for several days we were agonised: had we instead of helping the victim ended up further revictimising her? From this at least I learnt a major lesson: any activist intervention which tends to revictimise the victim is morally wrong and the concerned activities must bear full responsibility for atonement if that happens ...[6]

Some of the problems may have arisen because Mathura, like most other victims of custodial rape, occupied a class and caste position socially inferior to that of most IWM activists. The power relations between the activists and the victim remain an uncomfortable question, even where the two do not come into direct contact or confrontation, as in this case.

Another unresolved issue is that the anti-rape campaign, while it was essentially a challenge to the State, also asked the State to initiate legal reforms, such as banning a film that glorified rape. Would this give more power to the State, power which it could also use to silence radical movements? The contradiction between confronting the State and then, almost in the same breath, appealing to it to redress itself, is obvious.[7]

Finally, the focus on custodial rape meant that other forms of rape — rapes within the family, such as incest and marital rape — were not directly addressed. The authors of the open letter had suggested that marital rape be included within the rape law, an idea rejected even by some members of the IWM, on the grounds that it would not be used by women, and that it would endanger the family. Nor was the exclusive focus on penile penetration of the vagina as the definition of rape taken up as a point of debate. What does this tell us about the notions of female sexuality embodied in the rape law, notions that were perhaps shared by activists in the IWM? This is a question addressed in the next part of this paper.[8]

Debate on rape: the legislature

The issue of rape first entered the Indian legislative arena in 1982, during debates in the Lok Sabha (lower House of Parliament) following the anti-rape campaign, which led to the 1983 amendment. One can observe a pattern in these debates: platitudes about Indian womanhood are combined with the dread that rape unleashes in women within the family. One researcher suggests that the 1982-83 debates 'may be treated as an ethnographic source, indicating how the division between law/morality, rape/sexuality, chaste/unchaste, power/powerlessness (etc) played into the naming of rape as a juridical object in 1983'.[9]

The debates identify the Indian woman as a 'special' category, fit to be deified. A raped Indian woman bears a stigma of shame: 'If you want to protect the honour and dignity of the mothers and sisters of the country … let us give life imprisonment. Five to seven years' imprisonment is no punishment' (B Parulkar, 15.7.82, Lok Sabha Debates, p. 455 [hereafter L S debates]).

The deified woman within this discourse is a Hindu: 'Many of us, who believe in Hinduism, when we pray in the morning, we pray in the name of Ahalya, Draupadi, Sati, Tara and Mandodari' (B Parulkar, 15.7.82. L S Debates, p. 451).[10]

What happens to this Hindu woman of the collective fantasies of the Lok Sabha members once she is raped? She is rendered impure, unmarriageable: 'A rape victim … bears a stigma in the eyes of the society. She has to hide herself… So long as social attitude remains one of stigma of a victim of rape, the rape victim must be given compensation. If the victim can not look forward to a marriage, if she is unmarried (and) if she is married, in most cases, if not all' (Amul Datta, 21.11.1983, L S Debates, p. 424).

After defining the raped woman as a victim engulfed in shame, the discourse shifts to another plane, assuming that if she is not a 'good, virtuous' woman she cannot be raped. 'Bad' sexually promiscuous women routinely lie about rape, according to this logic, wanting to frame innocent 'respectable' men. To be a real victim, a woman must be moral and chaste. Regarding the clause that the 'consent' of a woman under the influence of liquor or other intoxicants will be held void, one member argued: 'Cases of self-induced intoxication ought to be excluded from this clause. In modern society and in even some backward societies where liquor and other intoxicants are freely consumed, false charges of rape can easily be brought' (B Parulkar, Dissenting Note, 'The Gazette of India Extraordinary', 2.11.1982, 32).

Another member held that '... after all, we are not dealing all the time with virtuous women, we may also deal with some who, unfortunately, do not conform to the normal standards of womanhood. A woman may be there who has first taken a lot of drinks herself voluntarily and intoxicates herself and then complains against the man and says: "Look! I never appreciated the nature and consequences of the act"' (Ram Jethmalani, 1.12.1983, L S Debates, p. 413).

Somewhere, the notion of the unchaste woman as being from a socially inferior caste and class also seeped in. For Mathura, a failure to acknowledge and respect different modes of sexual conduct in tribal and non-tribal society had led to her being branded promiscuous. Here too, the fear was that 'such' women may lie about rape, especially about rape by socially privileged men. A proposal by Geeta Mahajan and Susheela Gopalan that 'power rape', or 'rape perpetuated by taking advantage of economic domination or power', be put into the amendment, was rejected on these grounds ('Gazette of India Extraordinary', op. cit., p. 29). One felt that to criminalise 'rape by economic domination' would be counter-productive, as '... there will be instances where some unscrupulous women may take advantage of it and try to blackmail or may do some character assassination ... So, one should be very careful in this matter' (P. Venkatasubbaiah, 1.12.93 L S Debates, p. 412).

The law on rape does not recognise marital rape, and most in the Lok Sabha opposed its criminalisation. The man's right to rape his wife extends to child marriages, contradicting the legal prohibition of such unions. Rather, it was argued that child marriage laws should be effectively implemented instead of criminalising sexual relations between husband and wife. Some even argued that personal laws and customs of different communities be respected in this area:

Marriage is permitted, marriage is good, even if it takes place when it is an early marriage you recognise it as valid and provision prevents the man from becoming a hermit in the sense that you keep your wife in a cupboard and do not have sexual intercourse with her and she should not have sexual intercourse with you. This is absurd. It is surrender to a spirit which is not really secular (Ram Jethmalani 1.12.1983. LS Debates pp. 414–5).

While the rape law aims to protect a wife judicially separated from her husband, this may be nullified by the provisions in another law: restitution of conjugal rights, whereby the court directs the absconding spouse to reside with the petitioner. Failure to comply is a ground for divorce. Clearly, efforts to preserve the 'interests' of the patriarchal family are held paramount by the State.

While marital rape is recognised in Lok Sabha debates — mostly in terms of the rape of child brides — the rape of other children within the family is not acknowledged even as a possibility. If at all, the rape of children is recognised only as rape by strangers — and, in the terms of the debates, rape is the act that sexualises the child. The 1983 amendment 'fixed' the age of consent at 16 years, which was opposed by some Members of Parliament.

The reasoning is that the woman who is less than 16 years, though she gives her consent to sexual intercourse, cannot be said to understand the implication of it and the effects of it ... Is it not a fact that in the modern society the knowledge of sex is available to boys and girls who just enter their teens ... Some of them can be said to be past masters. It is a point to be reconsidered whether ... consent of a girl who has full experience and knows the enjoyment of sex, willingly has sexual intercourse with a man, the man should always be condemned (N.J. Shejwalkar, 'Gazette of India', op. cit. pp. 22–3).

Arguments verging on the racist emerge: 'In tropical countries, women mature somewhat early. The Muslim religion permits marriage on puberty. To outlaw all sexual intercourse under the age of 16 would lead to other evils which society ought not to encourage' (B. Parulkar, op. cit. p. 32).

Interpretations: the rape law and the judiciary

The rape law is based on a logic that benefits the offender rather than the victim. Some categories of rape are not legally acknowledged, such as non-penetrative forced sexual interaction, or marital rape. Others are sidelined and thereby dismissed, such as incest, or intra-family rapes. The sexual history of the woman continues to be significant both for the law and the judiciary, in addition to the extra-legal considerations of class and caste. This is reflected in a 1989 Bombay High Court judgement concerning a tribal woman who was raped by a police officer who entered her house at night on the pretext of conducting a search. It states that: 'Probability of the prosecutrix, who was alone at her hut, her husband being out, having consented to sexual intercourse cannot be ruled out. Benefits of the doubt must go to the accused and acquittals cannot be interfered with' (State of Maharashtra vs Vasant Madhu Devre, 1989 CLJ 2004).

Most 'progressive' judgements are made in favour of virginal young women, offering sympathy for her loss of virginity and her future marriage prospects. This is illustrated in a judgement concerning a girl under 16 years of age, stating that: 'the inherent bashfulness, the innocent naivety and the feminine tendency to conceal the outrage of masculine aggression … are the factors which lead to concealment by the girl.' The judge condemned rape as 'a bestial act of lust' (AIR 1980 SCC 1252). Converting the rape of a legal minor into an act of lust rather than one of violence leaves unquestioned the indiscriminate use of power by men — while attaching certain approved qualities to the hapless victim.

A major lacuna is the lack of separate provision for the rape of children within the family. Unlike many European countries and parts of the USA, child sexual abuse (CSA) is posed within the general category of rape. Incest does not even warrant a mention as 'aggravated' rape, unlike rapes within police custody or the rape of a pregnant woman.[11] As for an adult, penile penetration alone constitutes rape for a child. Yet any form of sexual assault is extremely traumatic, and to have a child conform to the exacting standards (that are unfair even for an adult woman) and close scrutiny that the rape law expects from a victim could only add to the trauma. For instance, children aged five years or less are subject to invasive medical examination. In one recent case, the examining doctor found the hymen of the five-year-old victim completely torn, with lacerations on all sides of her vagina. Concluding that the injuries could have been inflicted with an instrument like a piece of glass, the doctor suggested that it was 'doubtful' that rape was committed on the child. Instead, she was probably subjected only to indecent assault — a lesser charge. While the judge rejected this argument as 'unwarranted and perverse', what is remarkable is that it could be presented at all in a court of law. Somehow, the insertion of a piece of glass is considered legally less heinous than penile penetration, even for a small child (State of UP vs Babul Nath, SCC Vol.6, 1994, 26).

At the crossroads: the IWM and the issue of rape today

In September 1992, an employee of the State-sponsored Women's Developmental Programme was raped in her village in Rajasthan as a reprisal for her attempts to stop child marriage among the upper-caste Gujjars and Brahmins. The police and the judiciary successfully shielded the culprits, in spite of the campaign launched by the IWM, whose support marked a new phase in the movement. There is close contact with the victim, Bhanwari Devi, who belongs to the same struggle against oppression that many other women have been fighting. Her rapists were acquitted by the sessions court in November 1995, the judge basing his decision on two planks. One, a romanticisation of Indian culture, held that in India an uncle and his nephew could not jointly commit rape; that since the alleged rapists belonged to different castes, the rape was not possible; that Indian rural society would not degenerate to the extent that villagers would lose 'all sense of caste and class and pounce upon a woman like a wolf'; while Indian culture made it impossible that the victim's husband (a witness to the rape), 'who has taken a vow to protect his wife ... just stands and watches his wife being raped, when only two men twice his age are holding him'. The second plank was the more technical 'lack of evidence'.

The judgement caused outrage and disappointment in the IWM. The rapists were not only acquitted, but on grounds that were both untenable and unfair. The efforts to support Bhanwari's struggle continue, but her ordeal has also led to efforts by the IWM that are likely to have a long-term impact. A bill on sexual violence has been proposed by a feminist group and approved by the National Commission for Women and Children; and recommendations on sexual harassment in the workplace have been made to the Chief Justice of India by Saakshi, a Delhi-based women's group.

The bill states that: 'The present law [on rape] has become so outdated in terms of language and intent in that it fails to acknowledge the true nature of sexual assault crime. In particular, the existing law does not address the increasingly visible offence of child sexual abuse ... a substantial number of child sexual abuse cases are occurring within the family' (Sexual Violence Against Women and Children: An Act to Combat Sexual Violence Against Women and Children Draft Bill).

Seeking to re-define rape to include other forms of violence and violations faced by women and children, the bill includes a range of sexual activities to be criminalised if perpetrated against a minor (under 18 years) —with or without her consent—and against an adult without her consent. It includes the introduction by a man of his penis into the vagina, external genitalia, anus, or mouth of another person; the introduction by one person of an object or a part of the body into the vagina or anus of another person; touching, directly or indirectly, any part of the body of another person; uttering of any word, making of any sound or gesture, or exhibiting any object or part of the body with a sexual purpose. The proposed charge of 'aggravated sexual assault' includes assault by a police officer, a member of the Armed Forces, a public servant, or by anyone 'in a position of trust, authority, guardianship or of economic or social dominance' on someone 'under such trust, authority or dominance'. The medical examination and investigation procedures are also clearly stated.

Fixing the age of consent at 18 years was not an easy decision. One of the lawyers involved writes, 'Some members were concerned that if the age was as high as 18, then even consensual sex between adolescents in the 16–18 age group would be an offence. This position ... [is] highly puritanical and moralistic'. Ultimately, the age was fixed at 18 years, because that is the age when Indian citizens are first entitled to vote.[12]

Saakshi's recommendations address sexual harassment in the workplace. The rape of Bhanwari Devi is seen by many women as having happened in the course of her work; and it is the responsibility of the employer (here the State) to provide her with a safe working environment — which it clearly failed to do. The recommendations make the employer responsible for preventing sexual harassment in the workplace, and ensuring justice for the wronged woman. They suggest that the employers must raise the issue in an affirmative way; develop appropriate sanctions and disciplinary measures, including dismissal; sensitise all concerned; and expressly prohibit sexual harassment in the workplace.

Though important — and pioneering, in that no provision currently exists in Indian law prohibiting or criminalising sexual harassment in the workplace — these recommendations may not benefit most working women, since they cannot be implemented successfully except in the formal sector. Given the economic realities of India, as liberalisation pushes ever more women into the informal, home-based economy (where they are unsure who their 'real' employer is), the resolutions may be difficult to act upon.

The path ahead is long and rocky; but the IWM's understanding of the issues of rape and child sexual abuse has become increasingly complex over the last 20 years. While with Mathura the 'issue' took precedence over the victim, with Bhanwari Devi both are equally important. The shift from custodial rape alone to rapes of children and women within the family lends the IWM greater depth and focus. It also creates a continuum of empathy between the raped woman and others struggling for equality, justice, and freedom. As Bhanwari herself said during the 1995 National Conference of Women's Studies: 'My struggle is not for myself alone. It is a collective struggle for all the women who have been wronged. I will continue to fight.'

Notes

1 Flora Agnes, 'The anti-rape campaign: the struggle and the setback', in Chaya Datar, ed. (1993), *Violence Against Women*, Calcutta: Stree.

2 Vibhuti, Sujata, Padma, 'The anti rape movement in India', in Miranda Davis, ed. (1983), *Third World, Second Sex: Women's Struggle and National Liberation*, London: Zed.

3 Personal communication from Sandya Gokhale, *Forum Against Oppression of Women*, Bombay.

4 Manushi, Dec 1979 – Jan 1980.

5 Vibhuti et al., in Davis op. cit.

6 Upendra Baxi, *Inhuman Wrongs and Human Rights: Unconventional Essays*, New Delhi: Haranand (1994).

7 Vibhuti et al., op. cit. p. 184.

8 Baxi op. cit. p. 76.

9 Pratiksha Baxi, 'The Normal and the Pathological in the Construction of Rape: A Sociological Analysis', MPhil dissertation, Department of Sociology, University of Delhi (1995,), p 65.

10 Mythical Hindu characters, women known for their unstinting devotion to their husbands.

11 'Aggravated' rape refers to those categories warranting greater punishment (S376 PC): here, child rape is a category, but not intra-family rape in particular. The words used are 'rape on a woman when she is under 12 years of age', as if the act of rape would convert a child under 12 into a woman.

12 Ratna Kapur, *Introduction on the Proposed Law on Sexual Assault*, New Delhi: Saakshi.

■ **Geetanjali Gangoli** *is active with the Indian Women's Movement and works on a voluntary basis with the Forum Against the Oppression of Women in Bombay.*

This paper was first published in Development in Practice *Volume 6, Number 4, in 1996.*

Guatemala: uncovering the past, recovering the future

Elizabeth Lira

Editor's note: In early 1995, Dr Elizabeth Lira met with Guatemalan human-rights workers involved in the transition process being overseen by the UN (MINUGUA), and with the Human Rights Office at the Archbishopric.[1] In December 1996, the Peace Accords were signed, signalling the formal end to the 36-year old war; and, among other things, conferring amnesty on the military. The author's personal reflections on her visit are included here for the insights they offer into the human-rights dimensions of transition from war to peace.

Human rights: a numbing obsession

What does one expect of Guatemala, a country with one of the worst human-rights records in the western hemisphere? I had few preconceptions other than what I had learned through reading people like Rigoberta Menchú.[2] I knew that the military had pervaded all areas of life and expression, and had an idea of the Guatemalan version of 'national security' and the policies emanating from this. I had listened to Guatemalan refugees in Los Angeles, Berkeley, and Boston, and read many accounts of human-rights violations, torture, assassinations, and political disappearances.[3] I knew the work of the historian and poet Eduardo Galeano, and had read poetry and stories of the Mayan culture. Yet, in spite of everything I thought I knew, I had no idea of what Guatemala would actually be like.

My first impression of Guatemala City was the pollution. The traffic congestion is so severe that the City seems on the verge of collapse. Everything moves at a snail's pace. The constant racket is itself an assault on the senses: traffic, street sellers, music blaring out from stores and shops. This chaos is compounded by the posters, bill-boards, and signs of every shape and size hanging from every available space. The number of street sellers makes it impossible to move around. The beauty of the City is lost in the noise, the crush, the bustle, and the general disorder. But I saw no beggars, no violence. Everyone seemed friendly. The human climate was hard to decipher.

Some chance conversations gave some idea of what was going on in the country. I met a woman who was selling weavings, and who began telling me about the pains in her heart, which she described as one might describe anguish. She told me about her insomnia, her fears, her psychosomatic illnesses. It was not easy to ask her what caused these pains. But she told me that they had to do with profound fears and things to do with death concerning members of her family, 'things one cannot talk about'.

How many things can one not talk about in Guatemala? I tried to understand what was going on, but the newspapers gave very little idea. The television was the same. Though endless speeches by politicians appeared on the news, these were mostly repetitive and meaningless. Whatever their ideological persuasion, they seemed pretty much the same. Television itself seemed like a good way to create exactly the kind of confusion that would make sure that nothing ever changed.

Superficially, the human-rights issue seemed to be the most important subject in the public arena, given the exhaustive media coverage. It was disconcerting to see how 'human rights' could become so obsessively absorbing. Cases were denounced, extracts from reports on human rights in Guatemala were publicised, and so on. Many issues featured under 'human rights', from acts of violence attributed to the guerrillas, or the international report on human rights, to the discovery of clandestine graves or information about past violations. I wondered whether this almost indiscriminate coverage did not trivialise the problem, by making everyone used to hearing about atrocities that would be quite overwhelming if one stopped to listen, while at the same time mixing up politically motivated violence with acts of State-sponsored terrorism. A similar thing happened in Argentina when it came to light that gross human-rights violations had been committed by the Alfonsin government. Information was prolific and constant. What it actually generated was a sense of banality; people became weary and uninterested. Thus the enormity of the horror went unheeded. Consequently, the information had no great impact on public opinion, and there was little pressure to go beyond simply denouncing events.

Yet in Guatemala I was impressed by people's sense that these crimes had been committed with impunity, that the threat is ever-present. Fear is palpable, despondency as well as hope, and the impact of the violence is deeply personal. Given the scale of the atrocities, and how they are perceived by ordinary people, it is hard to understand how the peace process could be underway. Some say the transition began in 1985. But what can this possibly mean? The end of the repression? A transition to what? How can fear be eradicated? How can social peace be built? What social and cultural behaviour will be needed to make possible the changes in people's minds, alongside the political changes? What institutional changes will occur? How can the yearned-for information to establish the truth possibly be produced, given the impunity with which the abuses were committed? And what about the military? In other spheres, what would be the role of academics, what controls would be imposed on their teaching, and what type of ideological persecution might follow? What about the students or social organisations?

The signing of the Peace Accords will bring enormous consequences, especially for those who suffered most intimately the four decades of political violence.[4] Fear lies behind every conversation, like something woven into the fabric of society, something one must live with. Reading the Archbishop's reports on violations of human rights since 1992, I was impressed by the thoroughness of the documentation. I also realised that, while the scale has lessened, grave violations continue. Fear becomes a chronic response to a situation that is constantly threatening, and where there seem to be no boundaries. Arbitrariness is 'normal', even in a context that is supposedly democratic.

I was often told that the telephones were probably bugged, and correspondence intercepted. But it was far from clear what kinds of precaution one should take. Simply reading the denunciations made me feel that there were no adequate precautions, since political repression was characterised above all by being arbitrary and unpredictable. From what I could gather, the recent persecution had focused on people who had been trying to piece together the sheer enormity of the violence of the past, especially in the countryside. It was clear that some forces wished to stop cases reaching the tribunals, in spite of MINUGUA.

Breaking the silence

A central element in human-rights work is to contribute to peace through establishing what actually happened. Breaking the silence means creating the social conditions that enable the truth — 'the clarification of what happened in the past' — to contribute to a kind of subjective justice. This means that individuals must be able to see that their experience of pain and persecution is recognised by society.

For the Church, breaking the silence means restoring the value of human life, and re-weaving the social fabric so that it can live with a collective memory of the past: a past that includes not only the repression, but also resistance, and the efforts of the dispossessed to bring about social and political change. It is therefore developing a history of the violence in order to help build a Guatemala that can form a collective judgement about its past. This is not just a question of gathering statistics, but also of testifying to the ways in which the violence was experienced by individuals, families, and entire communities. This will in turn contribute to the work of the Truth Commission.

Basically, there two main aims to the ambitious task of recovering the collective memory. The first is to gather well-substantiated information that can serve as legal documentation, so that judicial proceedings may be intitiated. The second is to take first-hand testimonies that register not only the concrete facts, but also their psychological impact. The emphases are different. The rigour with which facts must be documented for strictly legal purposes may not generate the right conditions for recovering the collective memory, which is essentially intended to have a subjective and therapeutic function. Giving testimony is a chance to recount a history that has been silenced — and to do this to someone who represents that element of Guatemalan society which wants to acknowledge as fully as possible what really took place. Giving testimony is an emotionally cathartic act. However, while it can be a huge psychological relief for the individual, it is also important to contain these emotions — something that places a huge responsibility on the one who receives the testimony. This person must demonstrate empathy, but also be skilled in conducting the interview so that the witness is not re-traumatised. The interviewers themselves need to be trained and supported by a capable team. They need a high level of self-awareness, an understanding of what draws them to the work, their fears and vulnerabilities, and inner resources. It is important to bear in mind that, while the interviews are with individuals, the political repression was generalised, and much of the history is of wholesale massacres of rural indian communities.

The Church's task is then both social and political, but also potentially therapeutic. It is concerned with recognising and validating the experience of violence, of the pain and loss this caused, in a context that still cannot guarantee basic rights to all. A context in which the 'truth' is a repudiation of the military version of repression and the impunity the Armed Forces have enjoyed, and which is thus likely to generate intense emotional reactions. This remains an extreme experience that cannot be adequately symbolised.

At the same time, the interviewers are not immune to what they will be documenting, for the experiences and realities have been shared by almost everyone. Those who testify are likely to have needs that range from wanting to establish the truth and to seek justice, to simply having someone listen to them. Likewise, the interviewers will have their own needs and expectations of the process. These should be out in the open, so that they do not interfere with the work.

Who wants to hear about the past?

And what is this work? It consists in building up both a formal environment and the human relationships that will foster the gathering of reliable information. This means establishing a sense of trust, and a relationship that can 'hold' the torrent of emotional release. Fear will inevitably be present, since fear is a protective emotion, part of the protective baggage that is itself a response to the life-threatening reality in which everyone has had to function and survive for decades. At the same time, what people will describe is a history of unimaginable horror and suffering. Who wants to hear it? Who wants to tell it? What's the point of telling it? And why listen?

While all this can come to seem self-evident to those who are used to working with these issues, the answers are in fact not at all obvious. We need to be very clear with everyone concerned about why we are doing this work. We cannot deny the need for emotional release, as well as the support and feedback people will want: but *catharsis by itself is not enough.* The ways of providing such help may include therapy, or various forms of cultural expression. But what is needed is a space within which people can find some kind of symbol that can both bring together what they know about what happened, and their feelings about it, and gain a public recognition of the experience. This is fundamental, given Guatemalan society's denial of what took place, and the impunity with which these violations were committed.

Victor Montejo's *Testimony: Death of an Indian Community in Guatemala*, published in 1993, is a first-person account of the obliteration of an entire community, and gives some insight into the emotional issues to be taken into account. The personal vulnerability, and the possibility of reprisals for giving testimony about the repression, must be considered. It is one thing for someone spontaneously to talk about some of what happened, interwoven in a discussion about the price of maize or whatever, because it is a very deep and significant part of their everyday existence. But it is quite another to talk about these terrible events in a formal and structured way, for this to be registered, written down, recorded. People's reactions could be very different. For some, it will be something they have been longing to do for many years. Others may be more ambivalent. Language and the meaning of particular symbols will vary from one ethnic group to another, just as the reactions and needs of mothers and fathers, children, brothers and sisters, husbands and wives, will differ.

Assessing reality: risks and feelings

What is essential is to have a realistic picture of the human-rights situation today, and the likely future scenario, in order to distinguish the real risks, as opposed to those perceived by people with long experience of repression and violence. This will provide the basis for a better understanding of the social conditions in which the work of collecting testimonies will be done. It will also assist in developing appropriate strategies for coping with the uncertainty and constant threat, the difficulties and risks inherent in a chronic emergency. Recognising one's own strategies gives insights into the defence mechanisms used by others — such as black humour, psychosomatic complaints, inter-personal conflicts, or specific psychological responses such as denial, or dissociation. Such awareness makes it possible to give space to and validate other people's fears, their uncertainties, their anguish; and at the same time to recognise that everyone involved in this kind of work also has the right and the need to have their own feelings recognised — whether of tiredness, frustration, or impotence.

This calls for having one's feet firmly on the ground. There are ethical issues at stake, as well as subjective needs. In addition to training, those involved in gathering testimonies also need a strategy of collective support. For many people, this work inspires great hope, and represents something they have been longing to happen. But precisely because of these expectations, reality will be very hard: it is important to avoid unrealistic expectations, in order not to lose hope.

If the preparatory work is done collectively, it should be possible to anticipate specific situations, and predict the kinds of problem that will arise — difficulties affecting the indviduals involved in the work, or the people they are interviewing; problems inherent in the situation, or the process itself. If we know that we will be dealing with pain — pain that will often resonate with our own — we need to learn how to offer support, acceptance, emotional limits, and help. These are part and parcel of the work, and we need to be clear and self-aware in order to function. But there are more specific issues in learning how to ask questions almost as if one were taking a clinical history — which means being as objective as possible about what the patient says, without losing sight of the fact that it is pain that causes someone to be concerned about themselves, and to seek and accept help. Taking a clinical history is a skill that must be learned, but in this case it also entails both the interviewer and the 'patient' using all the resources at their disposal to relieve the pain that is actually caused by giving the history.

When we talk about memory, we are using a concept that is sometimes a metaphor for unresolved personal or collective grief. We need to construct memory, to recall — 'feel it in one's heart again' — in order gradually to close the wounds. There are two elements here: the history of the 'patient', and that person's history in his or her wider social context. That is, the history of the community, the family, the social group to which they belong. Therapy is often a process of restoring the link between an individual's grief and their collective experience. It is like finding some sense of what happened, whether as a way of understanding the past, or of projecting into the future. It does not depend on an outsider, but on each particular individual.

It is far from easy to see how to design an appropriate training programme for human- rights workers in this context. Clearly, the legal requirements are real, but have somehow to be combined with interviews which are intended to gather hundreds of profoundly painful experiences. The task of preparing people to deal emotionally and professionally with this is daunting. The needs of the coordinating team will differ from those of the people working on the ground, but there will undoubtedly be a need for some kind of counselling support for everyone in what cannot but be a gruelling experience. There is also the question of how to recognise psychological and psycho-social trauma, and how to formulate specific recommendations in response.

Underlying everything is a need to reflect on the wider implications of a 'transition' which seems to be focused on establishing peace and respect for human rights. This reflection should draw on a range of backgrounds and disciplines, and promote a meaningful exchange of experiences of other post-war transitions in order to get a sense of what is really possible, and where the problem areas lie. Perhaps the problems to concentrate on relate to political transitions, which depend on achieving peace. The calls for peace have many different origins, each posing a different challenge. In Guatemala, memory, history, truth, justice, reparation, and reconciliation have particular significance. Experiences of transition elsewhere would need to be set within the Guatemalan context, where real advances in the area of human rights are taking place, and where it has been the military who have been primarily responsible for political repression. Any such exchange should be within a framework for mutual learning from the experience of people elsewhere.

Human rights and mental health: some Guatemalan experiences

Many Guatemalans have for years been involved in mental health as well as human-rights work. One NGO began working in the early 1990s in areas that suffered badly in the war, using a small technical team and a larger group of community-based health workers. For them, mental health has nothing to with classifying people as mad, and shutting them away. It has to do with living communities, with collective identity, and with day-to-day survival. In this, small production projects play an important role.

The organisation CONAVIGUA (a war widows' rights organisation) was formed as a direct response to the repression, and provides a forum within which these bereaved women 'can say what we feel, talk about our fears, our mistrust, as well as domestic violence, and alcoholism'. Alcoholism has increased in the rural areas, which the army occupied and controlled for 15 years. Their festival of community mental health is aimed at helping people to see this as a collective issue that needs some public expression.

The case of the Nebaj area of El Quiché is telling. High in the mountains, about 250 kilometres from the capital, it suffered terribly from army repression and brutality. The military destroyed many homes and settlements, and then forced people to live in 'model villages', in each of which is a monument to military achievements — in what? creating peace? promoting education? repression? Given the lack of land in these 'model villages', the army eventually began to allow resettlement in the surrounding areas. The people of Nebaj, mainly young adults, began to return to their places of origin in the early 1990s. They did go back, while other communities were still resisting in the mountains. They had been forced to leave because of the massacres. They are dignified, interested in the world around them (for example about events in Chiapas), but do not place their trust lightly. The men urge the women to speak out, while the women hide behind their lack of Spanish, at least when they are addressing a group. Speaking to them individually is easier. Gradually, these people open up enough to speak about what they have been through. About how they are frightened to set down roots, because who knows whether the violence is really over, or whether it will return. They are afraid, and yet they seem quite calm under the protective shield of their own language. To see where these people are living now, to view the 'model villages', to understand something about how they organise themselves, and how they see their lives — all these details give shape to the personal testimonies of repression.

Back in the capital, some church-based human-rights workers are holding a workshop to look at the problems they face. One group mentions people's fear of denouncing any form of violence, whether personal or structural. They may show apathy and lack of interest in the institutions that are meant to deal with the problem. Other reactions range from timidity to aggressiveness, from despair to obedience, resignation, or passivity among those who have directly experienced political repression. 'They seem to have no recollection of what has happened, saying "I don't want to remember", while what one sees are signs of anguish, stress, disbelief, and despair.' A second group displays a range of reactions and behaviour patterns. People are afraid of widespread criminal violence. Some people are against human rights. Many of those who come to the human-rights office are aggressive, even violent, and expect to be given everything on a plate. But some become enthused, and start getting involved. A third group of workers describe how when people come to file a denunciation about a violation, they often find themselves weeping. Some fear that this may affect their capacity to work, others fear that they are not affected at all. The last group talks about violence in all its forms — economic, political, and social — seeing poverty as a consequence of this. 'People feel marginalised, and violence causes psychosomatic problems', they say.

In summing up, one worker says that many of the things they have described are things they feel themselves: 'We feel frustrated, impotent in the face of a situation of no change'. The group jokes about impotence, taking it to mean sexual impotence. Then someone comments that this is not so far from the truth, and that sexual impotence is one way in which people respond to their feelings of helplessness. 'We reproduce the authoritarian system as a kind of defence mechanism. We become withdrawn and express things through black humour and booze. Liquor is the people's psychiatrist' — a comment that causes ripples of nervous laughter — 'and may be a personal response to pressure.'

> We need to be on constant alert, not on the defensive, but ready to fight back. It is something we get very sensitive about, and sometimes aggressive, when we feel impotent, when we feel helpless and yet responsible for raising others' expectations. We think about our work all the time, and lose sleep over it. We feel indignant about things that can't be changed. We are afraid that our impotence may make us indifferent. We sometimes over-identify with the problems we hear about, and feel isolated as a result. The work is stressful, especially since some of us have been the direct victims of violence. It can give rise to a wish for vengeance, and this can become a very strong feeling among human-rights workers. The problems we are dealing with affect us. And what we don't talk about can come out later in the form of aggressiveness. The sources of stress stimulate our own destructive capacities, and we seem unable to tap into our constructive potential.

Collaboration through difference

This is only the briefest glimpse of Guatemala. But in everything I saw, observed, and heard are things that are familiar — from the constant traffic jams to what these human-rights workers said. But many things are very different. Any serious efforts to collaborate in the area of human rights must be based on a recognition of our similarities and our differences, and on the possibilities that these offer. In all human experience we find some elements that are universal, and others that are unique: and we must learn to recognise these. Can we work together on human rights? Possibly, but precisely in those areas in which we can join in identifying our differences, so that these become the basis for a genuine exchange of experience.

Notes

1 The Catholic Church was embarking on a nationwide effort to recover and record the memory of the military atrocities that took place throughout the 1970s and 1980s, and which resulted in the deaths of 150,000 over the 36-year war.

2 Rigoberta Menchú is a Mayan indian and human-rights activist, awarded the Nobel Peace prize in 1990.

3 As the opposition to the government represented by the URNG (Guatemalan National Revolutionary Unity) mounted in the late 1970s, the armed forces launched 'a campaign of terror that has rarely been paralleled for its savagery (and lack of publicity) in the history of Latin America. The resulting carnage was so vast that at least another 30,000 Guatemalans [had] been killed [by 1987], hundreds more [had] been "disappeared", 440 Indian villages [had] been wiped off the face of the map, and between 100,000 and 200,000 children [had] lost at least one parent' (J. Painter, 1987, *Guatemala: False Hope, False Freedom*, London: Latin America Bureau).

4 Since the CIA-sponsored military overthrow in 1954 of Jacobo Arbenz, the democratically elected President of Guatemala.

■ **Elizabeth Lira** *is a Chilean psychologist and political scientist with wide experience in situations of repression and violence in Latin America and elsewhere, including Bosnia. She is the Director of the Latin American Institute of Mental Health and Human Rights (ILSA).*

This paper was translated and abridged by Deborah Eade. The full version, in Spanish, is available on request.

Strengthening unions: the case of irrigated agriculture in the Brazilian north-east

Didier Bloch

Introduction

About half of the Brazilian north-east is occupied by the *Sertao*, a semi-desert area some three times the size of Great Britain, which is both very poor and densely populated. The region is, however, crossed by the San Francisco river, whose valley, especially around the towns of Petrolina and Juazeiro, has been the scene of huge socio-economic upheavals.

The first occurred in two stages, corresponding to the filling in 1979 and 1987 of two World Bank-funded hydro-electric dams: as a direct result, 100,000 people were displaced, some of whom became landless.

The second, more gradual, upheaval started in the mid-1970s with the decision to expand irrigated agriculture. Individuals and large private groups, attracted by the infrastructure put in place by the government, along with generous financial incentives, invested hundreds of millions of dollars along the banks of the San Francisco.

Two fruits, mangoes and grapes, soon met with considerable success in both domestic and export markets. The grapes that are found in British, French, and German supermarkets at Christmas time come from this part of Brazil. The vineyards provide significant employment: more than 15,000 labourers work there, the majority of them permanent and female. The other labour-intensive crops, for example tomatoes and onions, tend to have a variable contingent of workers, depending on the period, paid by day or by season during harvests.

All these developments, along with the influx of small peasant farmers fleeing the terrible droughts that ravage the *Sertao* every ten years, explain why Petrolina and Juazeiro have seen an unprecedented growth in their populations and economies over the last two decades.

New union strategies

These transformations have forced the rural workers' unions (which in Brazil are organised by municipality) to rethink their strategy in the Sub-Medio San Francisco. Initially focused on small farmers, they had first to mobilise their efforts to help the victims of the big dams, demanding their resettlement on new lands. From the early 1990s, the more dynamic of these set up specific structures to defend the rights of the increasingly numerous salaried workers in irrigated agriculture. Two unions in the state of Pernambuco (Petrolina and Santa Maria de Boa Vista) effectively took up the defence of these wage labourers, despite the fact that on the other bank of the river, in the State of Bahia, their opposite numbers carried on with clientilistic policies focused on small farmers.

After their defeat in 1991 during the first attempt to negotiate with the owners of the irrigated farms, the two unions decided at the end of 1993 to start a major education and mobilisation campaign among the wage labourers. This time they had two sources of support. On the one hand they had advisers, experienced lawyers and negotiators from the regional and national union federations. On the other, they received a small grant (US$6,300) from Oxfam (UK and Ireland), to finance an educational campaign on basic labour rights. This represented cash which they did not have, given the small number of workers actually unionised. Most of the workers are essentially poor migrants from the arid zones of the *Sertao*, for whom wage labour and irrigated agriculture are completely new.

A large mobilisation process preceded the difficult negotiation phase. Information meetings were organised at people's places of work and living quarters, as well as general assemblies in the two towns. Finally in February 1994, the first collective agreement in the San Francisco valley was signed: a significant occasion, which the Brazilian Minister of Labour attended in person. The agreement was valid for a year, and a new round of negotiation took place in February 1995, when new advances were made.

Improvements for wage labourers

So what are the results a year and a half after the signing of the first accord? In terms of the direct benefits for the workers, the most important is without doubt the increase in wages. In 1995, the permanent workers were getting a minimum salary plus 10 per cent, which is around US$110 monthly; and a decrease in irregular employment (the employers registering their workers more than in the past, thus guaranteeing them their basic social rights). Overall, the working conditions have improved, even though they remain far from the ideal, as we shall see.

As far as the unions are concerned, the benefits are also visible. Following the campaign, the number of unionised wage labourers more than doubled, rising from 1,400 to 3,500, of whom 2,500 regularly pay their subscription. In increasing their constituency, the unions have strengthened their financial autonomy. They also won free access to the farms at certain times for the union representatives; stable employment; and the right to two days' leave per month.

From Oxfam's point of view, a simple analysis of the ratio of costs (for Oxfam) versus the benefits (for the workers) demonstrates the multiplier effect of financing the campaign for the workers' rights. Following the 1994 campaign, about 20,000 workers each gained US$6.47 extra. (The net salary in 1993 was US$64.70.) Calculating on the basis of 13 months' annual salary, that makes US$1.68 million from financial support of US$6,300, representing a multiplier ratio of 1:267. Of course, Oxfam is not the only factor in the campaign's success. Apart from the dynamism of the unions, the end of the drought which assailed the north-east between 1990 and 1993 also contributed to the reduction in available labour, and thus helped in the negotiations. Oxfam's support was necessary but not sufficient to achieving the package of results.

Finally, it is important to mention the increasing number of women who are engaged in union activity, becoming union representatives and indeed leading the strikes. Apart from the fact that they are in the majority in the vineyards, it is the women who are particularly affected by forms of abuse, ranging from sexual harassment by the overseers to the dismissal of pregnant women and the latters' exposure to the spraying of poisonous products. Here again, Oxfam has played an advisory role, insisting that gender questions have a special treatment at the very heart of the union.

A limited victory

Though there have been some concrete gains, there is still much to be done. Firstly, despite the support of the Federal Labour Office, the majority of the clauses in the accord are not respected. For example, the spraying of toxic chemicals continues to be carried out during work hours, and there is often no drinking water available, thus obliging the workers to drink the polluted water direct from the irrigation channels.

Secondly, it is the permanent workers who have most benefited from the accord, though these are on fixed-term contracts. However, the great mass of day and seasonal labourers are very difficult to organise, particularly as many live several hundred kilometres away, making the return journey between their home areas in the *Sertao* and the banks of the river each year. Thus the most numerous and the most exploited category, the seasonal workers (and very often their children), is for the moment beyond the reach of the union. An illustration of this is the dreadful labour fair that draws together several thousand day-labourers on the outskirts of Petrolina. The work these people do in the tomato and onion plantations has been classed as semi-slavery by a regional newspaper not given to exaggeration.

Finally, the accord takes in only one bank of the river, on the Pernambuco side. On the other, in the state of Bahia, the situation has hardly changed. Indeed, there could be a negative impact: lower salaries in Bahia could encourage new business concerns to give preference to establishing there in the future.

Limits of the development model

Over and above the question of employment, one is faced with the development model itself. On this, the union's stand is ambivalent. While calling for agrarian reform, it is not putting forward any concrete proposal that takes into account the specific situation of the riverine region.

Let us go back to the problem of the wage labourers: what is a monthly salary of US$110 worth? In Brazil, it is just about enough to buy a basic food ration to meet the minimum nutritional needs of a family of four. In other words, it is a miserable salary. The 40 per cent of families in Juazeiro (population 130,000) who live in poverty are testimony to that.

Further, the great majority of workers who are 'lucky' enough to get this salary work in the vineyards. Their work depends on the employment of a large number, five per hectare, of poorly qualified and ill-paid people. A simple calculation based on the rate of productivity (30 tonnes per hectare per year over two and a half pickings) demonstrates that there is little scope for increases in the workers' wages. A monthly wage of US$200 for the employees would mean no profit for the owners. Further, some would assert that this method does not allow for the simultaneous production of a large quantity of good-quality grapes, so that exports are limited to the months of November and December, when Brazil has a monopoly of the world market. As far as the domestic market is concerned, purchasing power is limited and it is unlikely that there will be a large increase in sales of an inessential product such as grapes.

In short, whether it be grapes or other products, apart from the climatic and financial conditions in the region, it is the low wages that make it attractive to business. The unions can go on attacking the low wages and employment conditions, but they will always come up against the 'economic imperative'. This will be the case unless they can suggest other ways of organising production, or (better still) new options which are both economically viable and socially just.

Finally, we should mention the serious ecological threats faced by the region. Among the worst are the salination of the irrigated areas resulting from poor drainage, the pollution of the river from fertiliser and pesticides and increasing waste from urban areas, and the silting of the river brought on by deforestation of the bordering areas. Some experts are already talking of the death of the river, in other words its loss of commercial viability (irrigation as well as fishing and energy generation) within two or three generations. The potential loss of productivity, and thus employment, due to the salination of the soils, should concern the unions.

Conclusion

If we are really talking about strengthening the unions of the Sub Medio San Francisco, this should include giving them access to a range of information about international business, the agri-food business, restructuring of world production and irrigation techniques, and their long-term impacts on the environment, thus encouraging them to get beyond the level of immediate labour issues. This would require promoting real networking with other unions and NGOs working in the heartland of the *Sertao*. In effect, the absence of a serious programme for the 12 million rural inhabitants of these semi-arid lands, and the resultant migration towards the river and large urban centres on the coast constitute the fundamental problems of regional development.

Without information which would allow them to participate in defining and implementing new directions for development, unions and NGOs risk being left in the wake of a development model led by global economic forces, by the business-owning class in Brazil whose sole motive is profit, and by a government little inclined to discussion, from whom there is little hope of great efforts on the social or ecological front.

■ **Didier Bloch** *is a journalist and consultant to Oxfam-Brazil, and author of 'As frutas amargas do Velho Chico'.*

This paper was first published in Development in Practice *Volume 6, Number 4, in 1996.*

All rights guaranteed — all actors accountable: poverty is a violation of human rights

Grahame Russell

This paper is a call to organisations concerned with development, environment, social justice, and human rights to work more closely together. It calls for reflection, debate, and action to protect and guarantee all human rights, and argues that all actors should be held accountable for actions which contribute to their violation. But first, a poem by Leonel Rugama:[1]

The earth is a satellite of the moon

Apollo 2 cost more than Apollo 1. Apollo 1 cost plenty. Apollo 3 cost more than Apollo 2. Apollo 2 cost more than Apollo 1. Apollo 1 cost plenty. Apollo 4 cost more than Apollo 3. Apollo 3 cost more than Apollo 2. Apollo 2 cost more than Apollo 1. Apollo 1 cost plenty. Apollo 8 cost a fortune, but no one minded, because the astronauts were Protestant, they read the Bible from the moon, astounding and delighting every Christian, and on their return Pope Paul VI gave them his blessing. Apollo 9 costs more than all these put together, including Apollo 1, which cost plenty.

The great-grandparents of the people of Acahualinca were less hungry than their grandparents were. The great-grandparents died of hunger. The grandparents of the people of Acahualinca were less hungry than their parents were. The grandparents died of hunger. The parents of the people of Acahualinca were less hungry than their children were. The parents died of hunger. The people of Acahualinca are less hungry than their children are. The children of the people of Acahualinca are not born to be hungry. They hunger to be born, only to die of hunger.

Blessed are the poor, for, because of them, we send rockets to the moon.

It ought to be considered criminal in all jurisdictions — national and international — that, at the end of twentieth century, States and other powerful political and economic actors[2] have not taken the decisions and actions necessary to end systematic and historical violations of the wide range of human rights (economic, cultural, civil, social, and political) of huge sectors of humanity who struggle, survive, and die in varying degrees of endemic poverty and misery. Since World War II, many more people have been killed by malnutrition, hunger, and disease (that is, by the systematic violations of human rights) than by the combined effects of all the wars and repressive regimes which have systematically violated political and civil rights.

'Seventeen million people in developing countries die each year from such curable infectious and parasitic diseases as diarrhoea, measles, malaria and tuberculosis.'[3] Many times more people struggle and survive in conditions which perpetually violate their basic rights; even by World Bank estimates, more than three billion people 'survive' on a daily income of US$2, or less.[4] A disproportionate number of the victims of these violations are women, children, indigenous peoples, and other vulnerable social sectors. This suffering, caused by imposed conditions of poverty, is rarely analysed or understood as a violation of human rights.

UDHR — fiftieth anniversary

12 December 1998 marks the fiftieth anniversary of the Universal Declaration of Human Rights (UDHR), the most widely known international human-rights agreement. Governments, inter-government agencies (such as the United Nations), and national and international non-government organisations (NGOs) will to mark the date in various ways.

This anniversary should provide a time to celebrate the major advance in universalising the notion that all human beings have rights. Since World War II, tens of thousands of citizens' organisations have emerged to promote this notion, and to undertake education and advocacy work.

The importance of these advances cannot be understated. However, the fiftieth anniversary is a time to focus on important questions which governments, other international actors, and the 'human-rights movement' have yet to address properly.

All rights

Most human-rights work to date has focused on certain political and civil rights, to the exclusion of others and of many economic, social, and cultural rights.[5] This work has ignored the fact that the UDHR itself enshrines a broad range of economic, social, and cultural rights; implicitly, it has ignored the principle of international law that all human rights are indivisible.

Human-rights work has also avoided investigating the often organic relationship between poverty (the over-lapping violations of numerous rights) and repression (a systematic violation of certain political and civil rights). In many countries there has existed or continues to exist a vicious cycle of poverty and repression.

A common scenario is that poor people, together with workers for social justice and development, and religious workers, educate themselves about their rights. They then organise to protest and fight against the violations which characterise their lives. Then the State, often with the support of powerful private-sector interests and foreign governments, responds with repression, in order to preserve the undemocratic, unjust status quo.

The problem with much human-rights work is that, while it has investigated and denounced the use of repression (that is, violations of political and civil rights), it has not examined the prior violations of economic, social, and cultural rights, nor the wide range of actors who contribute to all violations.

All actors

Most human-rights work has aimed only at holding the State accountable for rights violations (political and civil, for the most part) which occur within its borders. The actions of other States and of inter-State and private actors often contribute directly and indirectly to a wide range of violations of human and environmental rights, whether in their home countries or elsewhere. Often acting with impunity, these other actors are rarely held accountable to those whose rights they may have violated.

An example of an inter-State actor contributing to human-rights violations would be that of the International Monetary Fund (IMF) pressing the government of a dependent, perhaps indebted, nation, to impose political, legal, and economic programmes on its people which will increase violations of their rights. An example of a non-State actor would be that of a transnational company or bank contributing through its actions, whether directly or indirectly, to violations of human rights in a foreign country. An example of a State actor contributing to human-rights violations in another country would be that of one which provided funding, training, and/or weaponry to a foreign government (and/or private-sector para-militaries) which was systematically violating the rights of its own people.

Investigating and determining the human-rights responsibility of other actors does not negate the responsibility of the State for its own contribution to such violations, but rather focuses attention on, and apportions responsibility to, all other actors who also play a direct or indirect part in them.

Whether or not the State was the only actor capable of violating or guaranteeing respect for the rights of its citizens in 1948, it is clear today that other actors have an equally great or even greater impact on human rights than do most existing nation-States. While the State will continue to play a central role in the affirmation or negation of citizens' rights, other actors must be held accountable to those citizens world-wide whose rights are often negatively affected by their actions.

It is incumbent on the wide range of development, environment, social justice, religious, and human-rights organisations both to understand, and to bring human-rights analysis and pressure to bear on, the many actors involved, holding each accountable for their proportion of responsibility for human-rights violations.

Challenges — common cause, common language

The fiftieth anniversary of the UDHR thus provides a focal point for creative activities in the North, South, East and West, designed to open debate and discussion on the numerous challenges before us. One such challenge is for organisations working on issues of human rights and development, environment, and social justice, at all levels, to work more closely together.

To see how human-rights work has been compartmentalised, we might take the example of 'defending the rain forest' in a country such as Guatemala. 'Environment groups' might focus on 'saving' the forest and the atmosphere, ignoring the reason why poor people of Guatemala are obliged to slash and burn forests just in order to survive; and ignoring how the actions of national and international actors, controlling the unjust economic and development model, contribute directly to the destruction of the environment.

'Development groups' might focus in turn on how the prevailing development and economic model creates and perpetuates poverty, but fail to analyse poverty as a systematic violation of economic, social, and cultural rights, which often leads, organically, to systematic violations of political and civil rights.

'Human-rights groups' might focus exclusively on the use of State repression (violations of political and civil rights) against activists working to end poverty (violations of numerous rights), ignoring the prior and systematic violations of economic, social, and cultural rights of the poor, and ignoring the fact that other actors (such as the international financial institutions and other governments) contribute directly and indirectly to the entire range of human-rights violations.

For these intertwined issues, the international human-rights regime does provide agreements, law, analysis, and language which can help to overcome the often false separations between these areas of work. But a cultural and political challenge, for all groups working on these inter-related issues, is to educate people about, and to overcome, the accepted 'truth' that 'there always has been poverty and there always will be': the view that poverty is somehow a natural (if lamentable) phenomenon, rather than the result of economic, legal, political, and military decisions taken by human beings, States, and their many different institutional actors. And it is also a basic challenge to make more funding available for groups who are working on the wide range of human-rights issues, and holding the many different actors accountable.

Conclusion

'Human rights work makes it clear that the wide range of violations are neither inevitable or natural, but arise from deliberate policies, decisions, and actions. In its demand for explanations and accountability, the human rights movement, conceived in the broad sense as set out in this article, exposes the hidden priorities and power structures behind the violations. Thus, addressing all rights, in terms of their economic, political and social context, and holding all actors accountable, constitute critical steps towards challenging the conditions that create and tolerate poverty.'[6]

There is much human-rights work to be done — at community, national, and international levels — to address and reform national and international legal, economic and political systems which remain profoundly unjust.

Now is the time for development, social justice, religious, human rights, and environmental groups to form working alliances to address these issues. Now is the time to plan creative educational and political activities to mark the date of the fiftieth anniversary of the UDHR.

Notes

1 A Nicaraguan man who was killed in 1978 in the struggle against the Somoza dictatorship, which was kept in place both militarily and economically by the USA. Translated by the author.

2 By 'other powerful political and economic actors', I refer among others to inter-government financial and commercial institutions (such as the World Bank, the International Monetary Fund, the World Trade Organisation, the proposed Multilateral Agreement on Investments, etc); to other states and their various military, security, economic, and aid agencies; and to private, non-government entities such as transnational companies, banks, and financial investment institutions.

3 UNDP, *Human Development Report 1997*, Oxford: Oxford University Press, p. 28.

4 Cited in *La Jornada*, a Mexican daily, 2 February 1998.

5 In recent years, real advances have been made in the field of rights for women and indigenous peoples: systematic violations have been dealt with, albeit not fully or properly, by a growing range of national and international human-rights institutions. Women's and indigenous people's organisations have contributed valuable critical analysis of the traditional, narrow focus of 'human-rights' work, pushing it to overcome cultural biases and move towards addressing all actors, and all rights.

6 This slightly altered passage is from 'Unleashing Human Rights to Address Global Poverty', an unpublished paper by Chris Jochnick, legal director of the Center for Economic and Social Rights.

■ **Grahame Russell** *is a Canadian human-rights lawyer, educator, activist and Director of Guatemala Partners.*

This paper was first published in Development in Practice Volume 8, Number 3 in 1998; an earlier version appeared in Third World Resurgence.

Collective memory and the process of reconciliation and reconstruction

Wiseman Chirwa

Introduction

Over the last five years, several African and Latin American countries have experienced major political changes. Civil wars have come to an end, autocratic and oppressive regimes have crumbled and have been replaced by democratic ones. A new political dispensation has been ushered in. As this process unfolds, and the culture of openness deepens, a number of questions come to mind. A special issue of the *Index on Censorship* (Volume 5, 1996) raised several such questions concerning the relationship between truth, reconciliation, and the process of national healing: can people divided by civil war, torn apart by hatred and mutually inflicted atrocities, made sick by terror and oppression, heal themselves? Can nations, like individuals, be reconciled to their past and be cured of their ills by working through traumatic events, by telling and hearing the truth? Whose truth is it? Can nations cleanse their past and start again? More important, perhaps, can they ensure 'never again'?

These and similar questions were at the centre of the discussions at the Symposium on conflict-related issues, sponsored by Oxfam (UK and Ireland) and the Centre for the Study of Violence and Reconciliation, held in Johannesburg in June 1996. Of particular interest to the participants were the various ways adopted by communities and States in Africa and Latin America to achieve some form of reconciliation, healing, and reconstruction.

State-backed strategies for uncovering the truth

On the legal and political fronts, countries like South Africa and Rwanda have set up Truth Commissions to investigate the past and 'to facilitate a truth recovery process' so as to establish 'as complete a picture as possible of the causes, nature, and extent of past abuses' (Hamber, 1995). In Chile and Argentina, truth commissions 'arose in the context of new governments making a transition from dictatorship to civilian rule', while in El Salvador and Guatemala they emerged as part of the negotiations for transition from civil war to peace (Edelstein, 1994; see also Hayner, 1994 and 1996).

The understanding is that the process of truth- recovery will result in some kind of psychological healing. If victims of violence and other forms of rights-abuse are left without knowing the truth, or the opportunity to recount their experiences, they will remain traumatised and shattered. They will feel vulnerable and helpless and will have 'a distorted picture of society and humanity' (Hamber, 1995). Without truth there is no justice; and there is the danger of repeating the old mistakes. Thus, despite the differences in their mandate, scope, and approach, truth commissions are generally viewed as a starting point for national reconciliation and reparative measures (Edelstein, 1994: 5).

Truth commissions are not the only way of dealing with the past. Compensation tribunals and other mechanisms of reparation have been set up, for example in Malawi, to requite victims of abuse and as part of the process of promoting national reconciliation. A war-crimes tribunal has been set up in Rwanda, and some perpetrators of injustice during the apartheid regime in South Africa have appeared in court. These processes are among the ways of providing legal redress to victims, recognising the responsibility of the State, acknowledging the rights and interests of the victims, and raising public consciousness (ibid: 3). The last is an aspect of collective memory.

The participants at the Symposium felt the need to distinguish between the local communities and the State in this process. Truth commissions, compensation tribunals, and war-crimes tribunals are usually, though not always exclusively, State strategies for creating collective memories. They require a legal framework for their operation and a State bureaucracy for implementation. How then do local communities in the countries that do not have legal provisions for the setting up of truth commissions deal with their past? The available evidence suggests that they have devised their own ways. Sometimes supported by non-State agencies, and operating outside the State structures, they have embarked on the process of creating their collective memories to facilitate the process of healing, reconciliation, and reconstruction.

Alternative strategies

A good example here is the case of the Recovering the Historic Record Project (*Recuperación de la Memoria Histórica*, REMHI) in Guatemala, started by the Catholic Church (see Linsmeier, 1995; Hayner, 1994). This was designed to document testimonies from those who, in various ways, witnessed or were victims of the violence in the country from the 1960s. The testimonies would be submitted to the Truth Commission set up by the government. They would also be 'given back to the people in the form of pastoral statements to study and discuss. Thus begins what will be a long process of reconciliation' (Linsmeier, 1995:5). Several rural communities also embarked on the exhumation of the mass graves of the 'scorched earth' massacres of the 1970s and 1980s. The exercise was aimed at recognising the lives of those who were brutally murdered, giving them a proper burial and the reverence they deserve; to 'clarify the truth of what had happened', and to let 'the government, the military and the world realise that there is a law in Guatemala, and that justice must be served' (ibid). The new graves will serve as a reminder both to the government and the local communities of the atrocities of the past, so that any repetition of those events is avoided.

The Guatemalan exhumation exercise and the documentation of memories through interviews serve as good examples of how societies, independent of the State, deal with the past and the problems of reconciliation and healing.

Another illustration of a local group that has taken the initiative on its own to create a collective memory is that of the *Madres de la Plaza de Mayo* (Mothers of May Square) in Argentina. Ingo Malcher (1996:132) reports that 'every day the mothers [members of the group] meet here to continue their 20-year struggle, begun during the military dictatorship (1976–1983), to establish exactly what happened to their disappeared sons and daughters and to demand retribution against those who imprisoned, tortured and killed their children'. Documents, oral accounts and various other forms of evidence are examined and put together to establish a comprehensive account that can provide clues to what happened. It is worth noting that the 'mothers' refused to accept monetary reparation, because 'they felt that the state was buying their silence rather than social and historical recognition' (Hamber, 1995; see also Malcher, 1996). They want 'truth and justice', and an end to impunity, not money.

The case of Malawi

Similar exercises are planned, and some are indeed being undertaken, in Malawi. Victims of State murder have been given proper burial and memorial services, and a history project to document and publicise past abuses has been proposed by a group of scholars at Chancellor College, the country's main university campus. It aims to collect testimonies from both victims and perpetrators in various parts of the country; and publish popular works on these for use in schools, religious organisations, and other institutions. The dissemination of the results will also be undertaken through newspaper articles and radio and video documentaries.

On their own, communities in some parts of Malawi are making home videos and documentaries of their experiences under the dictatorial regime of Dr Hastings Kamuzu Banda. Lists of detainees and those who 'disappeared' have been drawn, showing the dates when they were picked up by the police (where the information is available), where they were detained, when they died or came out of prison, what happened to their family members, and other details of that nature. These have been submitted to the History Project proposed by the scholars at the university. The country's Compensation Tribunal has also collected voluminous accounts from victims of abuse. Members of the History Project are now requesting the Tribunal to allow them to document and preserve these accounts properly and professionally, so that they become an authentic record of the past for use by the present and future generations.

The Project is also proposing the establishment of local museums where artefacts of victims — personal belongings, pictures, and works — and those of the perpetrators of abuse would be preserved and displayed to the public. The weapons used by the perpetrators, and other tokens of State oppression, would also be housed in these museums, to provide symbols of the local communities' pride and identity, and to raise public consciousness. The museums would also become historical sites, an attraction to tourists, and thus give greater publicity and recognition to the victim communities. Lack of funding has delayed the implementation of this Project.

The case of South Africa

In South Africa, Christian organisations and non-government organisations (NGOs) are also actively involved in creating, documenting, and preserving collective memories. A good example is the Practical Ministries of the Christian Development Agency for Social Action. Some issues of its publication, *Practical Ministries*, have carried accounts of past abuses and the personal experiences of the victims (see, for example, *Practical Ministries* Volume 1, No. 1, Jan–March 1996). The organisation has also provided material support to those who suffered. Homes that were destroyed by politically motivated violence have been re-built, and relief supplies and facilities such as safe water have been provided to the victims of forced removals and those of post-apartheid political violence. According to Cosmas Desmond (1996), '"practical ministries are setting out to show that, given appropriate assistance, even the most devastated community can rebuild itself"'.

The *khulumani* (speak out) groups in South Africa are another practical example of how collective memory is created, documented, and preserved. These are groups of the victims and/or relatives of victims and sympathisers who regularly meet to discuss their experiences. They also map out the strategies to follow in engaging the government in detailed consultations on issues of justice, reparation, and physical protection. The emotional support provided by the members of these groups to each another serves as psychological therapy in the process of reconciliation.

Collective memory: some questions

It should be noted that collective memories have some shortcomings. To begin with, how collective are 'collective memories'? Whose memories are they? There is always the danger that the memories of the victims will take precedence over those of the perpetrators. Individuals are also good at suppressing some of their memories and highlighting and emphasising those that might be attractive to their sympathisers. As Michael Ignatieff (1996) has rightly observed, 'peoples who believe themselves to be victims of aggression have an understandable incapacity to believe that they also committed atrocities. Myths of innocence and victimhood are powerful obstacles in the way of confronting unwelcome facts.'

The memory becomes collective when it goes beyond an individual account, subscribed to and shared by a group. It must have historical and emotional relevance, connecting seemingly discrete events in a cause-and-effect manner. An account of a simple event that has no historical and emotional relevance is not collective memory. It becomes so when it invokes shared emotions and consciousness. It is for this reason that collective memory becomes part of the process of healing, reconciliation, and reconstruction at both the individual and communal levels.

However, the connection between collective memory and national reconciliation is rather unclear. Ignatieff (ibid) has further observed that we vest our nations 'with consciences, identities and memories as if they were individuals'. 'But', he asks,

> ... do nations, like individuals, have psyches? Can a nation's past make people ill as we know that repressed memories sometimes make individuals ill? Conversely, can a nation or contending part of it be

reconciled to its past, as individuals can, by replacing myth with fact and lies with truth? Can we speak of nations 'working through' a civil war or an atrocity as we speak of individuals working through a traumatic memory or event? ... If it is problematic to vest an individual with a single identity, it is even more so in the case of a nation (ibid).

The participants at the Symposium considered that collective memory can be an effective tool for reconciliation and healing for individuals and local communities. The examples cited above are ample evidence for this. It may not be fully effective for the nation as a whole. But these examples also show how local communities, on their own, acting independently of the State, deal with their past; and how they work towards the declaration: *nunca mais*—never again!

References

Desmond, Cosmas (1996) 'Rebuilding homes, restoring hope', in *Practical Ministries,* vol. 1, no. 1, pp. 4–5.

Edelstein, Jayni (1994) 'Rights, Reparations and Reconstruction: Some Comparative Notes', *Seminar Paper no. 6. Centre for the Study of Violence and Reconciliation*, Blaamfontein, South Africa.

Hamber, Brandon (1995) 'Dealing with the Past and the Psychology of Reconciliation: The Truth and Reconciliation Commission, A Psychological Perspective', Public Address Presented at the Fourth International Symposium on The Contributions of Psychology to Peace, Cape Town, 27 June 1995.

Hayner, Priscilla (1994) 'Fifteen Truth Commissions — 1974 to 1994: A Comparative Study', in *Human Rights Quarterly,* vol. 16, no. 4, pp. 597–655.

Hayner, Priscilla (1996) 'Commissioning the truth: further research questions', in *Third World Quarterly*, vol. 17, no. 1, pp. 19–29.

Ignatieff, Michael (1996) 'Articles of faith', in *Index on Censorship*, vol. 5, pp. 110–122.

Linsmeier, Alice (1995) 'Documenting memories: the Church helps reconciliation in Guatemala', in *The Mustard Seed,* Fall, pp. 1–8.

Malcher, Ingo (1996) 'No truth, no justice', in *Index on Censorship*, vol. 5, pp. 132–6.

■ **Wiseman Chirwa** *teaches at the University of Malawi, and is involved both in training activists and parliamentarians in human-rights issues, and in documenting the experience of State repression in Malawi.*

This paper was first published in Development in Practice *Volume 7, Number 4, in 1997.*

Devastation by leather tanneries in Tamil Nadu

J. Paul Baskar

Leather tanneries have multiplied in Dindigul district, in the heart of the southern state of Tamil Nadu, India, over the last decade. There are already 76 units in operation, and the government has issued licences for 14 more. What was initially welcomed by local people as a source of potential employment is now being looked upon as a menace — a cancer which must be excised if the district is to be saved.

Nobody knows why the tanneries came to Dindigul district in the first place. Tanning is a water-intensive industry requiring enormous quantities of fresh water. Every 100 kilograms of skins tanned use 3,200 litres of fresh water. Yet Dindigul has traditionally been a drought-prone area. With the groundwater-table being low, farmers must already depend on tank irrigation for their crops. These same tanks became the basic water source for the tanneries as well, in addition to bore wells, all of which further lowered the water-table. The result was a virtual drying up of all water sources for agricultural purposes.

The process originally employed for tanning was a harmless one, in which certain locally available leaves and herbs were used. This was a time-consuming process, taking 40–45 days to complete. With the increase in demand for finished leather, most units switched to the chrome-tanning process which involves a variety of chemicals: lime, sodium carbonate, sodium chloride (common salt), sodium sulphide, sulphuric acid, ammonium sulphate, chromium sulphate, fat, liquor, oil, and dyes.

Raw skin and hides are received in the tanneries in wet salted or dry salted condition. The salt, which is used as a preservative, is first removed, and the skins then subjected to various processes, including soaking, liming, airing, fleshing, and de-liming, followed by washing and tanning, using vegetable material. In the chemical process, after de-liming, the skins are dated and pickled before being chrome-tanned. The chemical process takes barely three days and is therefore preferred. All but a handful of the tanneries in Dindigul employ the chrome-tanning process.

Predictably, the water used in the tanning process is discharged as waste water, mixed with chemical effluents. The biggest pollutant is common salt (at the rate of three to four tonnes for every 100 tonnes of hides tanned), with sulphide and chromium compounds contributing to a lesser extent. Mixed with these liquid effluents are a number of noxious solid wastes. This polluted water from the tanneries in Dindigul district is discharged into the open, without any treatment whatsoever. And the water which fails to penetrate the soil to contaminate groundwater makes its way through canals to the large irrigation tanks in the area. Even the water which the rains bring to these tanks gets contaminated by these poisonous wastes, which can otherwise be seen as dried-up patches on the tank beds.

Of the 568 tanneries in Tamil Nadu, the 76 in Dindigul employ about 3,000 workers in all, more than 50 per cent of whom are low-paid child labourers—from a total population of nearly 200,000. Thus, the claim that the tanneries provide employment to local people, put about by the industry's proponents, is unsubstantiated. Far from improving the economy of the region, the tanneries of Dindigul have succeeded only in playing havoc with the lives of the local people.

The units process about 17,200 skins every day, making the area one of the biggest exporting centres of finished leather in the country: the annual export earnings from the region are over Rs 200 crore (Rs 2,000,000,000). In the process, over 500 lakh (50 million) litres of polluted water are discharged each day from the tanneries. Each tannery contaminates groundwater within a radius of six kilometres. The combined effect of contamination from the untreated effluents on the local inhabitants can easily be calculated. People used to cultivate several crops, but, with the advent of the leather works, agriculture progressively diminished. Most families sold their lands to the tanneries. Today nothing grows on the fields. Deprived of a means of livelihood, many people were forced to apply to the tanneries for employment.

The effluents from the tanneries form stagnant pools, and their stench is quite unbearable. The presence of salts far in excess of tolerable limits results in the withering away of standing crops (including full-grown palm trees), while seedlings just do not germinate. The tanning industry has not merely devastated the land, but has also upset the intricate biological food chain of the area: fruits, crops, and even fish, in the few tanks that have not dried up, have perished. The extent of effluent pollution can be gauged from the fact that even the milk of tender coconuts bred in the area has an unmistakable salty tang.

People in the area suffer from a variety of ailments: constant stomach-ache, headache, dizziness, and diarrhoea. A study conducted by the Peace Trust—a Dindigul-based voluntary organisation active on this issue since 1988 — indicates that, in addition to instances of leprosy, cases of tuberculosis and night blindness were substantially more numerous among the people in the area than was normal. There was also an unnaturally high incidence of abortions and miscarriages, and at least five cases of sterility in two of the worst-affected villages.

According to a spokesperson from the Peace Trust: 'We have found that in 13 villages, as many as 1,090 houses have been damaged due to pollution. Only 208 have remained unaffected. A total of 817 acres of wet, dry, and uncultivated lands have been laid to waste by the pollutants. Eight large tanks which irrigated vast tracts have become totally dry. Drinking-water drawn from 350 of the 367 wells has become unusable. What is more, over a period of one year, when our study was conducted, there were as many as 135 abortions and 76 still births in the 13 villages. We came across 561 cases of chronic headache, 94 cases of diarrhoea, 10 cases of leprosy, 19 cases of tuberculosis, 49 cases of chronic cough, and 88 cases of night blindness. The workers and employees of the tanneries also constitute a high-risk group. Only a few units provide employees even with rough rubber gloves and protection for the feet, improvised out of used rubber tubes. Since a large number of the workers are child labourers, the protection proves woefully inadequate and most workers suffer from contact dermatitis and a string of other disorders.'

Members of the Tanners' Association of Dindigul admit that there is much truth in the findings of the Peace Trust. However, they claim that the discomfort of the local people is a small price to pay for the benefits which accrue to society at large. They cite the substantial export potential of finished leather for the Indian economy. According to them, the tanneries are a direct source of employment to about 3,200 people directly and to over 7,000 families indirectly. Any attempt to close down the tanneries can be construed, they feel, only as a step against development.

However, there is no denying that the drawbacks, in human terms, far out-weigh the benefits. P.N. Bhagwati, former Chief Justice of India, addressing a seminar on the Dindigul situation, said: 'A healthy environment is a funda-mental necessity, and the right to live should be interpreted as the right to live in such an environment.' Claiming that the ecological crisis required equal or even more concern than the economic crisis facing India today, Bhagwati stressed the importance of establishing district-level 'green courts' to deal with air, water, and soil pollution and other ecological disturbances. Environ-mental protection, he emphasised, is not necessarily opposed to development.

The Peace Trust organised a string of protests in the form of processions and fasts by affected villagers. It was only in December 1989 that M.M. Rajendran, then Chief Secretary of Tamil Nadu, promised a delegation from the Trust and Dindigul Environment Council (promoted by the Trust) to look into the long-standing problem and initiate necessary action. Consequently, in March 1990, the Government of Tamil Nadu announced approval of a common effluent-treatment plant for Dindigul at a cost of Rs 270 lakh, of which 15 per cent was to be contributed by tanners and tannery owners in the form of shares bought, while the Central and State Governments were to contribute 25 per cent each. The balance of 35 per cent was to be raised in the form of loans from financial institutions. The effluent plant was expected to deal effectively with the sludge from nearly 40 major tanneries in the area. Since the effluents were to be carried in tubes to the central pollution treatment plant, contamination of the soil and groundwater would be minimised. Two disused irrigation tanks, Sengalkulam and Chenkulam, together occupying 50 acres, were located for setting up the plant. One more plant was also sanctioned at Rs 270 lakh.

However, one year later, nothing further has been done towards constructing the plant, and the people of the affected villages around Dindigul continue to reel under the malign influence of the effluents. Similarly, a scheme to provide potable water to the affected villages in order partially to mitigate the problems of the people is yet to start working.

The establishment of a couple of effluent-treatment plants and the provision of drinking water will not in themselves ease the situation. The continued issue of licences has to be stopped, and all tanneries strictly made to follow pollution-control norms. In addition, steps will have to be taken to reclaim the already ravaged earth. Biologists suggest the planting of *atriplex numalaria*, more commonly known as the salt bush, which is known to desalinate fields in a period of six to eight years, making them ready for cultivation. Only then will the havoc wrought by years of chemical devastation be undone.

But whether the governments, both Central and State, have the will to take up such an obviously daunting task remains to be seen.

■ **J. Paul Baskar** *is the Chair of the Peace Trust, whose address is Opp. Police Housing Colony, Trichy Road, Dindigul 624 009, Tamil Nadu, India.*

This paper was first published in Development in Practice in Volume 2, Number 2, in 1992.

Annotated bibliography

The concept of universal, indivisible, and inalienable human rights remains a highly contested one. Debates on empowerment, and on the relationships between social diversity and social and economic exclusion, have also influenced current thinking on (human) rights and (human) development. The cutting edge of much thinking on such issues necessarily takes place at the level of national organisations which are themselves engaged in the defence and promotion of rights and development. This Bibliography offers a sample of classic and contemporary writings on these broad themes, and lists some of the major international agencies which serve as reference points in the field of human rights. It was compiled and annotated by Caroline Knowles with Deborah Eade, Reviews Editor and Editor respectively of Development in Practice, *with assistance from Miloon Kothari.*

Books

Gudmundur Alfredsson and Katarina Tomasevski: *A Thematic Guide to Documents on the Human Rights of Women: Global and Regional Standards Adopted by Intergovernmental Organizations, International Non-governmental Organizations and Professional Associations*, Martinus Nijhoff, 1995
A systematic presentation of international human-rights standards. A broad range of treaties, declarations, recommendations, codes of conduct, model legislation, ethical, professional, and technical standards is presented thematically, and substantive standards are reproduced, rather than full texts. The book includes main policy documents (UN and Regional), main global human-rights instruments, and thematic chapters on elimination of gender discrimination, labour rights, social rights, the right to health, rights of the girl child, violence

against women, women with disabilities, administration of justice, humanitarian law, and refugees.

Philip Alston (ed.): *The Best Interests of the Child: Reconciling Culture and Human Rights*, Oxford: Clarendon Press/UNICEF, 1994

The 1989 UN Convention on the Rights of the Child is the world's most widely ratified treaty. Focusing on such diverse issues as child custody in South Africa, education in Egypt, the evolution from traditional customary law to modern family law in societies such as Tanzania and Burkina Faso, the status of the child in South Asian societies, the interpretation of the child's best interests in the UK and France, and the Japanese education system, papers in this volume, edited by a leading authority on human rights, use the Convention as a lens through which to examine the relationship between different cultural values and the aspiration to achieve human-rights standards.

Amnesty International: *A Guide to the African Charter on Human and People's Rights*, London: Amnesty International, 1991

The charter (also referred to as the Banjul Charter) was adopted by Heads of State and Government of the Organisation for African Unity in 1981, and entered into force in 1986. It is unique in several ways: it deals in one document with civil and political rights as well as with economic, social and cultural rights; it sets out the obligations of human beings as well as their rights; and it deals with the rights of peoples as well as those of individuals.

Abdullahi Ahmed an-Na'im and Francis M. Deng (eds): *Human Rights in Africa: Cross-Cultural Perspectives*, Washington DC: Brookings Institute, 1990

This books presents 13 essays by philosophers, human-rights lawyers, and sociologists. Despite well-documented violations of human rights by governments, the editors maintain that many peoples and cultures worldwide uphold the dignity and worth of the individual and the values and principles of international standards on human rights. They reject, on empirical and normative grounds, the characterisation of human rights as a 'Western' concept, find that the tension between relativism and universalism in relation to human rights is a creative one, and argue for cross-cultural fertilisation and mutual reinforcement.

Zehra F. Arat: *Democracy and Human Rights in Developing Countries*, Boulder: Lynne Rienner, 1991

A study of the democratisation processes, and the common vacillation between democratic and authoritarian regimes. Synthesising the theories of modernisation, dependency, and bureaucratic authoritarianism, the author explains this instability in terms of the imbalance between the two groups of rights: civil-political and socio-economic. Arguing against the view that the latter are group rights which can be maintained only at the expense of individual, civil-political rights, or *vice versa* — and that a compromise between liberty and equality is inevitable — the author demonstrates that the stability of democracy requires a balance between the two generations of human rights. A historical review, and empirical analysis of annual measures of 'democracy' in over 150 countries, and case studies of Costa Rica, India, and Turkey support the thesis that nations which recognise civil-political rights and establish democratic systems fail to maintain them if they neglect socio-economic rights.

British Medical Association:*Medicine Betrayed: The Participation of Doctors in Human Rights Abuses*, London: Zed Books, 1992
An authoritative account of the responsibilities of physicians in protecting human rights, this provides a thoughtful ethical commentary, an overview of international law relating to torture and medical experimentation, and practical guidance for medical practitioners and policy-makers. The context in which doctors may commit gross violations of human rights is itself often conditioned by fear, ignorance, or extreme coercion. The Working Party which prepared this book confronts controversy and dilemmas head-on, and makes a number of challenging recommendations.

Ian Brownlie:*The Human Right to Development*, London: Commonwealth Secretariat (Human Rights Unit Occasional Paper), 1989
The concept of the right to development as a human right was proposed by Keba Mbaye in 1972, and was adopted in 1986 in a UN General Assembly Resolution as an 'inalienable human right'. This study examines the background and substance of its components, and its rationale. The full text of the Declaration is included with a commentary on each article.

Theo C. van Boven: *People Matter: Views on International Human Rights Policy*, Amsterdam: Meulenhoff, 1982
A collection of the author's main policy statements made before UN bodies, UN seminars, and in other meetings, while director of the UN Division of Human Rights from 1977 to 1982. The first section includes statements to various UN bodies, and the second section includes seminar and meeting statements on apartheid, new international order, fundamental freedoms, children's rights, human rights in Africa, unjust international economic order, and discrimination against indigenous populations. The recurring theme is that, in the end, it must always be the people who matter.

Noam Chomsky:*World Politics, Old and New*, London: Vintage, 1994
A distinguished scholar of linguistics, Chomsky is more widely known as a relentless critic of all forms of contemporary imperialism, and of US foreign policy in particular. His early indictment of US involvement in Vietnam and Cuba was followed by similar critiques of its role in Central America, the Middle East, and the Horn of Africa, and as a Cold War superpower. Common to Chomsky's prolific output is a concern with human rights, and with exposing the negative global impact of Western notions of liberal democracy in the context of its defence of corporate might.

Rebecca J. Cook (ed.):*Human Rights of Women: National and International Perspectives*, Philadelphia: University of Pennsylvania Press, 1994
This book asks how human rights can make a difference in the lives of women, given

that the very idea of human rights implies universal application. The authors argue that any attempt to address the human rights of women must consider how these can be protected in the context of women's own culture and traditions. The book looks at how international human-rights law applies specifically to women, and seeks to develop strategies to promote equitable application of human-rights law at the international, regional and local levels.

Theresia Degener and Yolan Koster Drese (eds):*Human Rights and Disabled Persons: Essays and Relevant Human Rights Instruments*, Dordrecht: Martinus Nijhoff, 1995
The UN Decade for Disabled Persons (1983-92) set standards and created the need to evaluate the relevant human-rights instruments for disabled people. This book offers a collection of in-depth essays, and an extensive compilation of international and regional human-rights instruments, guidelines, and principles of relevance to disabled people. It aims to serve organisations of disabled persons as well as governments worldwide as a resource and introduction to the issue, to dispel the notion that disability is a welfare issue rather than a human-rights issue.

Kathryn English and Adam Stapleton:*The Human Rights Handbook: A Practical Guide to Monitoring Human Rights*, Colchester: The Human Rights Centre, University of Essex, UK, 1995
Intended as a practical guide to relief and development workers, this book sets human rights in their international legal context and provides guidance on how to contact and make use of human-rights networks, how to monitor human rights and document, investigate and report violations, as well as ideas for how to lobby and apply pressure on governments and international bodies.

Ximena Erazo, Mike Kirkwood and Frederiek de Vlaming (eds):*Academic Freedom 4: Education and Human Rights*, London: Zed Books/World University Service, 1996
Fourth in a series of reports on specific countries' failures to deliver rights to education, on abuses of people's rights in the educational sector, and infringement of academic freedom and university autonomy. This volume offers an overview of the international standards of academic freedom, and spells out the obligations of States to guarantee educational rights. Showing the wide range of obstacles to full realisation of the right to education, several chapters analyse how disinvestment has undermined this right, particularly for women and minorities when structural adjustment programmes go hand in hand with stricter government control (including censorship) of universities and other educational institutions. Other reports show why globalisation and the existence of highly educated refugees demand a wider international recognition of educational qualifications.

Richard Falk:*On Humane Governance: Towards a New Global Politics*, Cambridge: Polity Press, 1995
In the context of economic globalisation and its political and social consequences, the sovereign State has a diminished role in shaping the history of humanity and so

dominating geopolitics. The main market- and capital-driven forces which constitute a political challenge to the State remain largely concealed. The author calls for a commitment to 'humane' geo-governance, i.e. a set of social, political, economic, and cultural arrangements committed to rapid progress in these five areas. This will depend on dramatic growth of transnational democracy, the extension of primary democratic processes, an evolving allegiance to global civil society, and the plausibility of humane governance as a political priority.

William F. Felice: *Taking Suffering Seriously: The Importance of Collective Human Rights*, Albany NY: State University of New York Press, 1996
Examines the evolution and development of the concept of collective human rights in international relations. Focusing on the tension between the rights of individual members of society and the collective rights of certain groups, the author argues that the protection of human dignity requires an expansion of our understanding of human rights to include those collective group rights often violated by State and global structures. He advocates a move towards a world in which decision-making is based on norms of basic human needs and true equality.

Susan Forbes Martin: *Refugee Women*, London: Zed Books, 1992
The author examines five areas which are central to all refugees' well-being: protection; access to social and material services; economic activity; repatriation and reconstruction; and resettlement in a third country. Challenging the common view that efforts to achieve gender equity are an unaffordable luxury in emergencies, the author offers a range of gender-sensitive policy and practice alternatives for each area.

David P. Forsythe (ed.): *Human Rights and Development: International Views*, London: Macmillan, 1989
This book challenges the conventional wisdom that the fate of human rights is determined by economic forces and conditions. The major theme is the space for political choice which determines the implementation of internationally recognised human rights, in the context of historical, social, and economic forces. Examines work done in the private sector in support of human rights (with chapters from Mexico, Nigeria, India, Norway, and the USA); the public sector (by authors from the Netherlands, Germany, Canada, and the USA); country studies (Turkey, Sudan, India, and Bangladesh); and an overview of the process of development and human rights.

Johan Galtung: *Human Rights in Another Key*, Cambridge: Polity Press, 1994
Best known for his work in peace studies, Galtung argues here that the human-rights tradition offers significant means to reduce global violence, although it needs recasting in order to achieve this. The Western historical and cultural imprint on the idea of human rights leads to theoretical and political difficulties which Galtung assesses, focusing in particular on the failure of the legal tradition to take account of problems which are rooted in the economic and political structures of society and culture. He develops an accounting approach to human rights, based on human needs, analysis of political, economic and social structures, and an examination of social and cultural processes.

David Held (ed.):*Prospects for Democracy: North, South, East, West,* Cambridge: Polity Press, 1993

An overview of theoretical debates about democracy, of the diverse circumstances in which it has developed, and of the conditions which are likely to affect its development. Contemporary interest has often conceived of democracy in terms of liberal democracy, has assumed that it can be applied only to 'governmental affairs' and has no place in economic, social, and cultural spheres, has presupposed that the nation state is the most appropriate locus for democracy, and has assumed that democracy is a Western achievement and sustainable only under the cultural conditions of Western lifestyles. This book challenges these assumptions and advances the debate on the future of democracy.

Charles Humana:*World Human Rights Guide,* Oxford: Oxford University Press, 1992 (first published 1983 then 1986)

A survey of 104 countries and 40 indicators from the major UN treaties, featuring those human rights which can be defined and measured, with regional maps of human rights throughout the world. The limited authority of the UN and its inability to impose on its member-states respect for its own treaties and principles means that public knowledge of human-rights abuses comes mainly from other sources. Monitoring and dissemination of information is the most effective way of applying pressure to regimes perpetuating human-rights crimes. The 1986 edition of this book formed the basis of the Human Freedom Index in the UNDP *Human Development Report 1991*, which described it as 'the most systematic and extensive coverage' of the classification of human rights.

Thomas B. Jabine and Richard P. Claude (eds):*Human Rights and Statistics: Getting the Record Straight,* Philadelphia: University of Pennsylvania Press, 1992

This book addresses how statistical methods and the statistical profession can contribute to the advancement of human rights, and is intended for a wide readership: government officials, scientists, members of human-rights advocacy groups, and others. The authors hold that it is not enough to know that violations occur; one needs to know which rights are being violated, how frequently, and who the victims and violators are. To evaluate efforts to advance human rights requires knowledge of how patterns of violence evolve. An important function is to let the world community know what the problems are, so that deliberate abusers of human rights can be held responsible. Chapters have been selected as illustrations of good statistical practice in the field, and there is a guide to human-rights data sources as an appendix.

Joanna Kerr (ed.): *Ours By Right: Women's Rights as Human Rights,* London: Zed Books/North-South Institute, 1993

Twenty-four essays, all by well-known authorities, call attention to the various forms of women's oppression and women's efforts to advance their rights by lobbying, legal reform, and the transformation of social attitudes. The book advances efforts to secure rights for women within the family: to own and inherit property; to exercise reproductive choices; to vote; and to move about freely without male permission.

Rajni Kothari: *Rethinking Development: In Search of Humane Alternatives*, New Delhi: Ajanta Publications, 1988

Explores the meanings of poverty in its economic, social, and political aspects and analyses the role played by the State and the market, both nationally and internationally, in the deepening of poverty. The author also examines the phenomenon of disempowerment and the declining access of the poor to the power structures of society. The author's concept of humane governance is introduced in this book and its companion *Transformation and Survival: In Search of Humane World Order* (1988).

Smitu Kothari and Harsh Sethi (eds): *Rethinking Human Rights: Challenges for Theory and Action*, Delhi: Lokayan, 1989

A collection of essays by Indian scholars and human-rights activists on issues concerning the nature of civil liberties, democracy, and the political and practical challenges facing human-rights movements, including an influential paper by Upendra Baxi entitled 'From human rights to the right to be human: some heresies'.

Edward Lawson (ed.): *Encyclopaedia of Human Rights*, Washington: Taylor and Francis (with UNHCHR), 1991

This reference book, compiled by a former deputy-director of the UN Division of Human Rights, includes detailed entries on international instruments having a bearing on human rights and fundamental freedoms; international organisations which promote and protect those rights and freedoms; practical ways by which international, regional, and national bodies promote, monitor, and supervise the implementation of human rights; and reviews of human rights in 165 countries and States. It includes the complete official texts of some 200 international standard-setting instruments; all entries are cross-referenced.

Mahmood Monshipouri: *Democratization, Liberalization and Human Rights in the Third World*, Boulder: Lynne Rienner, 1995

Abrupt democratisation does not always result in enhanced human rights. The author argues that human rights in fledgling democracies are most likely to be improved if the transition from authoritarianism is preceded by a process of economic and political liberalisation, which works as a prelude to a gradual expansion of civil society. The book uses democratisation, liberalisation, and human-rights studies to explain the frequency with which democratic processes in the Third World have been aborted. The analysis is supported with a comparative assessment of the progress in Algeria, El Salvador, Pakistan, and Peru.

Christopher A. Mullen and J. Atticus Ryan: *Unrepresented Nations and Peoples Organisation: Yearbook*, Dordrecht: Kluwer, 1997

Contains information about the 50 members of the Unrepresented Nations and People's Organisation (UNPO), created in 1991 to provide a platform for those nations, minorities, and peoples who are not represented in established international fora such as the UN. Its mission is to assist these peoples to advance their interests through non-violent means. The Yearbook provides an overview of UNPO's activities, a review of the history and current positions of UNPO members, a selection of key UNPO documents and annual information, as well 1996 Conference and Mission Reports.

Winin Pereira: In *humanRights: The Western System and Global Human Rights Abuse*, Mapusa: The Other India Press (in association with Apex Press and Third World Network), 1997
A passionate and scathing account of how, while having the potential to inspire and mobilise people to fight for social justice, the supposedly universal human-rights discourse and legislation serve the neo-colonial interests of Western capitalism, and are often used both to justify its project for global hegemony and to mask abuses perpetrated by Western powers.

Anne Phillips: *Engendering Democracy*, Cambridge: Polity Press, 1991
The author analyses liberal democracy, participatory democracy, and forms of civic republicanism from a feminist perspective. She looks at various forms of female exclusion from full citizenship, and the dilemma of whether to seek greater equality within an inegalitarian system or to work for long-term radical change; and at the retreat into 'personal politics' and small-group identities as a reaction against concerns about 'false universality'. The author's critique of democracy is as relevant to debates on civil society and 'good governance' as it is to attempts to promote 'gender-sensitive' development and relief work.

Majid Rahnema with Victoria Bawtree (eds): *The Post-development Reader*, London: Zed Books, 1997
A highly diverse compilation of 40 theoretical and 'bottom-up' critiques of development by several generations of political thinkers and activists from around the world, including Amilcar Cabral, Arturo Escobar, Gustavo Esteva, Orlando Fals-Borda, James Ferguson, Eduardo Galeano, Rajni Kothari, Serge Latouche, Ashis Nandy, James Petras, Wolfgang Sachs, Marshall Sahlins, Vandana Shiva, and Hassan Zaoual. Extracts and text-boxes are organised in five parts: The Vernacular World; The Development Paradigm; The Vehicles of Development; Development in Practice; and Towards the Post-development Age. The volume is indexed and includes an extensive bibliography.

Jamil Salmi: *Violence and Democratic Society: New Approaches to Human Rights*, London: Zed Books, 1993
While violations of human rights continue all over the world, Western criticisms and campaigns often present them either in a Cold War context or with what some people in the Third World see as an anti-Third World bias. This not only undermines their political impact, but implies that the human-rights record of Western societies is almost blameless. Here, Salmi develops a new conceptualisation of human rights which goes beyond the Western liberal tradition and provides a broader classification, applicable to any society. Thus it encompasses not only cases of clear and direct violence, such as torture, but also situations where violence is disguised and indirect: environmental threats, racism or sexism, and the alienating effects of unemployment.

Gerald Schmitz and David Gillies: *The Challenge of Democratic Development: Sustaining Democratization in Developing Societies*, Ottawa: North–South Institute, 1992

Democracy has an important role to play in maintaining a level of rights awareness, and continued efforts must be made for rigorous conceptualisation and analysis. The first section of this study defines the relationship between democracy and development (elements of democratic development, achieving and securing democratic political development, sustainable forms of democracy and development), and the second section looks at democracy in developing countries. Key themes and issues include building civil societies; gender, empowerment, and development; democratic trends in Africa, Asia, and the Americas; case studies from Senegal, Indonesia, Brazil, Guatemala, Nigeria, Sri Lanka, the Philippines; and implications for Canadian aid and foreign policy.

Henry Schue: *Basic Rights: Subsistence, Affluence and US Foreign Policy*, Princeton, NJ: Princeton University Press, 1980

This famous book argues for a universal right to subsistence and for basic rights as everyone's minimum reasonable demand upon humanity. Physical security is the first basic right, since in its absence all others become meaningless. Minimal economic security or subsistence (including unpolluted air and water, adequate food, clothing, shelter, and minimal preventative public health care) is the second basic right, and liberty (the right to social participation, freedom of movement, and due process) is the third. The author then discusses affluence and responsibility, responding to the objection that meeting subsistence rights places too great a burden on others who have the duty to honour them. The role of aid in development is also examined, and the author looks at some priorities and policy changes for US foreign policy which are required by the recognition of basic rights.

The South Centre: *Facing the Challenge: Responses to the Report of the South Commission*, London: Zed Books in association with The South Centre, 1993

When it was launched in 1990, *The Challenge to the South* (the Report of the South Commission) offered a detailed analysis of the problems facing the countries of the South. This book is a companion volume of 33 commentaries on the Report, corresponding to the South Commission's wish to supplement and expand its work through public comment and debate. It contains a summary of the Report itself, and includes essays by leading intellectuals and activists, as well as senior IMF and World Bank officials.

Rudolfo Stavenhagen: *Ethnic Conflicts and the Nation State*, Basingstoke: Macmillan Press in association with UNRISD, 1996

The author examines the construction and politicisation of ethnic identities and explores the wide-ranging policies suggested by scholars, and implemented by governments, to contain or resolve ethnic tension. The book provides an overview of how the current world situation has changed, and the character and evolution of ethnic politics, and it points out the dangerous implications of the concept of ethnicity in a world with high levels of migration, globalisation, and multiple identities. It is based on 15 case studies, carried out under the UNRISD research programme on Ethnic Conflict and Development.

Katarina Tomasevski: *Between Sanctions and Elections: Aid Donors and their Human Rights Performance*, London: Pinter, 1997
Building on earlier ground-breaking work, the author here reviews human-rights policies of individual donor governments and the European Union, through a selection of case studies in three decades: Cuba, Rhodesia, South Africa and Israel in the 1960s; Uganda, Chile and Ethiopia in the 1970s; Turkey, Burma and China in the 1980s. Other books by the same author include *Development Aid and Human Rights Re-visited* (1993) and *Women and Human Rights* (1993).

United Nations: *The Universal Declaration of Human Rights* (1948) (available in several languages)
Adopted and proclaimed by the UN General Assembly in 1948, this represents a major touchstone in human-rights discourse and legislation: the belief that all human beings are born with equal and inalienable rights and fundamental freedoms. The UDHR is legally binding on all UN member states. Over the last 50 years, its evolution and enactment have depended on numerous international conventions and treaties, each of which must be ratified individually by each member state. The Convention on the Elimination of All Forms of Discrimination Against Women (CEDAW), for instance, has been fully endorsed by 139 countries but 90 member states have either not signed or have expressed reservations.

UNDP: *Human Development Report*, New York: OUP (available in nine languages, including Arabic, French, and Spanish)
Published annually since 1990, this is a unique and comprehensive guide to human development worldwide. The first report, *Concept and Measurement of Human Development*, introduced the controversial Human Development Index (HDI), against which all nations are ranked in terms of their people's basic human capabilities. Fearing that this would be used by donors as a form of conditionality, the G-77 pronounced the HDI 'a very western view of human rights', arguing that it failed to recognise social and economic achievements in countries such as Cuba. However, successive Reports have consistently stressed the synergism between economic performance, political freedoms and representation, and social equity on the one hand, and respect for basic human rights on the other. UNDP also produces documentation on human rights and development in view of its role in mainstreaming human-rights issues throughout the UN system.

UNICEF: *The State of the World's Children*, Oxford: Oxford University Press
An annual report on development through its impact on children, offering a critical analysis of development policy and practice from the perspective of children and their needs. Recent issues have focused on the need to eliminate the 'apartheid of gender', and on the devastating effect of 'pain now, gain later' macro-economic policies on the health and well-being of children and their families. UNICEF's *Implementation Handbook for the Convention on the Rights of the Child* (1998) is a

practical tool for human-rights workers which analyses each article of the Convention, and gives details of relevant provisions in other international instruments, and examples of implementation from countries around the world.

Gregory J. Walters: *Human Rights in Theory and Practice: A Selected and Annotated Bibliography,* Lanham, MA: Scarecrow Press/Salem Press, 1995
This bibliography presents works published in English between 1982 and 1993, with extensive annotation for each entry. An introductory essay gives a history of human rights, and the thematic sections include introductory information sources; philosophical foundations of human rights; cultural relativism and cross-cultural perspectives; human rights and religious traditions; basic human needs, development and security; human rights and foreign policy; international law, organisation and human rights; group rights and individual rights; women's and human rights; emerging human-rights issues; teaching human rights; researching human rights. The UDHR and the 1993 Bill of Rights and Responsibilities for the Electronic Community of Learners are included as an Appendix.

Claude E. Welch and Virginia A. Leary (eds): *Asian Perspectives on Human Rights,* Boulder, CO: Westview Press, 1990
Exploring ways in which cultural preconceptions and practices influence individuals' rights, this book highlights significant human-rights issues through case studies in South and South-East Asia. The first section gives an overview of the international and regional context, and the second section examines Asian cultural traditions and human rights, including essays on Islam and universal rights; caste in India; and a Buddhist response to the nature of human rights. The third section discusses conflict, especially issues of ethnicity, class, and gender in the region; the fourth consists of a selected bibliography.

World Bank: *World Development Report,* Oxford: Oxford University Press
An annual publication and policy statement on a critical issue in development, which synthesises the thinking of one of the world's most influential financial institutions and grant-making bodies. Recent reports have taken the themes of poverty, employment and globalisation, and good governance.

Journals

Development in Practice: published quarterly by Oxfam GB, ISSN: 0961-4524, Editor: Deborah Eade.
A forum for practitioners, policy makers, and academics to exchange information and analysis concerning the social dimensions of development and humanitarian work. As a multi-disciplinary journal of policy and practice, it reflects a wide range of institutional and cultural backgrounds and a variety of professional experience. Other titles in the Development in Practice Reader series include *Development and Patronage,* which discusses the unequal relationships of power inherent in the development process.

Health and Human Rights: published quarterly by the François Bagnaud Center for Health and Human Rights, Harvard School of Public Health, ISSN: 1079-0969, Editor: Jonathan Mann.

An international journal dedicated to studying the relationships between human rights and health. The journal examines the effects of human-rights violations on health; the impacts of health policies on human rights; and the inextricable nature of the relationship between the promotion and protection of health and the promotion and protection of human rights.

Human Rights Quarterly published by the Johns Hopkins University Press, ISSN: 0275-0392, Editor-in-Chief: Bert B. Lockwood Jar.

A comparative and international journal which aims to help define national and international human-rights policy by providing decision-makers with insight into complex human-rights issues. Interdisciplinary in scope, the journal presents current work in human-rights research and policy analysis, reviews of related books, and philosophical essays probing the fundamental nature of human rights as defined by the Universal Declaration of Human Rights.

Netherlands Quarterly of Human Rights published by Kluwer, ISSN: 0169-3441 (editorial address: Jankerkhof 16, 3512 BM Utrecht, The Netherlands).

Contains scholarly articles on important issues of human rights in the world and the promotion and protection of human rights in international law. The journal also contains news on recent developments in intergovernmental and regional organisations and reprints texts of major international agreements, treaties, and declarations. Once a year it features a list of ratifications for all States of the world.

Peace Review: A Transnational Quarterly, published by Carfax Publishing Limited, ISSN: 1040-2659, Editor: Robert Elias (editorial address: *Peace Review*, Peace and Justice Studies, University of San Francisco, 2130 Fulton Street, San Francisco CA 94117, USA).

A quarterly, multi-disciplinary, transnational journal of research and analysis, focusing on the current issues and controversies which underlie the promotion of a more peaceful world. Peace research is defined very broadly to include peace, human rights, development, ecology, culture and related issues.

Organisations

Amnesty International: One of the world's largest membership organisations, with national chapters in many countries, AI works for the release of prisoners of conscience, fair trials for political prisoners, and an end to torture, extra-judicial executions, 'disappearances', and the death penalty. An authoritative and impartial source of information, AI produces country reports and other occasional and regular publications.

Food First Action Network: A network with members in 45 countries working to defend the right to food, especially through access to land and other productive resources, protection of the environment, adequate incomes, and secure employment. FIAN believes that hunger and malnutrition are not caused by food shortage, but by human-rights violations. It documents such violations and supports legal case-work, co-ordinates international and national campaigns, and promotes education and training programmes on economic human rights.

Habitat International Coalition: A coalition of over 200 NGOs from 56 countries working in housing and related subjects. Its members work together in international campaigns and share information, supported by a small secretariat, currently based in Mexico. The secretariat works with members to fight evictions, to promote the 'bottom-up' approach to housing, and to lobby governments and international agencies to recognise the right to adequate shelter with basic infrastructure and services.

Human Rights Information Network: Founded in 1976, Human Rights Internet is an international network and clearinghouse dedicated to serving the information and networking needs of the human-rights community. It publishes directories, the *Human Rights Reporter* to index and abstract all publications received in its documentation centre, and the *Human Rights Tribune*, a quarterly magazine which addresses human rights from an NGO perspective.

Human Rights Watch: Dedicated to protecting the human rights of people around the world by investigating and exposing human-rights violations, supporting victims and activists, and enlisting public support for human rights. Publications include a quarterly newsletter, the *Global Report on Women's Rights*, and an annual *World Report*. The 1998 Report provides a review of human-rights practices in 65 countries, the degree of freedom with which local and international organisations monitor human rights, and the role played in promoting or inhibiting human rights by the international community, particularly the UN, the USA, and the European Union.

International Centre for the Legal Protection of Human Rights (Interights): An international centre which focuses on the protection of human rights through legal remedies. Activities include providing legal assistance before tribunals; filing briefs in cases which raise issues concerning the interpretation of fundamental rights before national and international courts; advising on legal matters; and providing information on recent developments in human-rights law through *Interights Bulletin* (ISSN: 0268-3706).

International Committee of the Red Cross: ICRC's role is to protect and assist the victims of international and civil wars and conflicts. It is recognised as a neutral humanitarian agency in the Geneva Conventions and their Additional Protocols, which accord ICRC's delegates special authority. Its operations are conducted confidentially, and any abuses are raised privately with the controlling authorities. The ICRC takes a prime role in developing International Humanitarian Law, and has a wide range of publications, in English and in French.

International Council on Social Welfare: A worldwide non-government membership organisation of groups concerned with a wide range of issues relating to social welfare, including human rights, employment, and the design and provision of effective and equitable social services. ICSW has made follow-up of the 1995 World Summit on Social Development its central priority, and produces *Social Development Review* as well as other occasional publications.

The International Labour Organisation: Uniquely made up of representatives of governments, commerce, and organised labour, the ILO is the UN agency which seeks the promotion of social justice and internationally recognised human and labour rights. It formulates international labour standards, setting minimum standards of basic labour rights: freedom of association, the right to organise, collective bargaining, abolition of forced labour, equality of opportunity and treatment, and other standards across the entire spectrum of work-related issues. Publications include an annual report, educational and campaigning material on issues such as child labour and workers' rights, and research on international labour issues and standards.

Minority Rights Group: Promotes the rights of ethnic, linguistic, and religions minorities, and publishes brief and authoritative reports on minority-rights issues worldwide, both thematic and specific.

OCMT/SOS-Torture: The World Organisation Against Torture was established in 1986 to respond to the needs of local NGOs based throughout the world and to consolidate their efforts to raise international awareness of torture. It acts as a clearinghouse capable of reacting instantaneously to urgent cases, anywhere in the world. The SOS-Torture Network consists of 200 member organisations, each of which is established in advocacy for human rights in their country or region.

Oxfam GB: Publishes a wide range of books and monographs on issues arising from its own experience in taking a rights-based approach to development and humanitarian relief. *The Oxfam Handbook of Development and Relief* (1995) details the background to human-rights discourse and the legal and institutional mechanisms for addressing abuses; and offers a similar account of international humanitarian law in relation to armed conflict. Other relevant titles include *The Trade Trap: Poverty and the Global Commodity Markets* (rev. 1996*), The Oxfam Poverty Report* (1995), *Women's Rights and Development* (1995), *Economic Growth with Equity* (1998), and *Accountable Aid: Local Participation in Major Projects* (1998). *Making Her Rights a Reality*, published by Community Aid Abroad (Oxfam in Australia), is also available through Oxfam GB.

Office of the UN High Commissioner for Human Rights: (UNHCHR — formally known as the UN Centre for Human Rights.) Produces a number of important publications including the *UN Reference Guide in the Field of Human Rights* (1993), the *Official Records of the Human Rights Committee* (an annual survey), and a series of fact sheets dealing with human-rights issues which are under active consideration or of particular interest. The fact sheets (over 20 titles) offer a good account of human rights, what the UN is doing to promote and protect them, and the international machinery available to help realise those rights. UNHCHR's website maintains regular postings of current reports, resolutions, and other documents of major importance to human-rights activists.

UNESCO: Focusing on how to go beyond simplistic approaches to economic growth and modernisation, the UNESCO programme on culture and development stresses the importance of grounding development programmes and projects within the cultural systems which give meaning to people's lives and enable them to articulate their concerns and aspirations. UNESCO also publishes directories of development organisations, including the *World Directory of Human Rights Research and Training Institutions* (fourth edition, 1998).

UNHCR: The UNHCR website is an important source of information for human-rights activists. It provides on-line access to UNHCR's Newsline Service and Country Updates, and information about publications, including the annual report *The State of the World's Refugees* and quarterly magazine *Refugees*. Access is also available to Refworld, a collection of full-text databases of UNHCR documents, UN documents, legal information, and reference material.

Addresses of publishers and other organisations listed

Ajanta Publications, 1-UB Jawahar Nagar, Bangalow Road, Delhi 110007, India.

Amnesty International, 99-119 Roseberry Avenue, London EC1R 4RE, UK. Fax: +44 (0)171 833 1510. Website: http://www.amnesty.org/

Amnesty International Dutch Section, Keizersgracht 620, 1017 ER Amsterdam, The Netherlands. +31 (0)20 624 0889.

Apex Press, 777 UN Plaza, Suite 3c, New York NY 10017, USA. Fax: +1 (914) 271 6500.

The Brookings Institute Press, 1775 Massachusetts Avenue NW, Washington DC 20036, USA.

Carfax Publishing Company, PO Box 25, Abingdon OX14 3UE, UK. Fax: +44 (0)1235 401550.

The Clarendon Press, Walton Street, Oxford OX2 6DP, UK.

James Currey Publishers, 73 Botley Road, Oxford OX2 0BS, UK. Fax: +44 (0)1865 246454.

Food First Action Network (FIAN), PO Box 102243, 69012 Heidelberg, Germany. Fax: +49 (0)6221 830545. Website: http://www.fian.org/

Harvard Human Rights Program, Pound Hall 401, Harvard Law School, Cambridge MA 02138, USA. Fax: +1 (617) 495 1110.

Harvard School of Public Health, 8 Story Street, 5th Floor, Cambridge MA 02138, USA. Fax: +1 (617) 496 4380.

Habitat International Coalition, Cordabones 24, Colonia San Jose Insurgentes, 03900 Mexico DF, Mexico. Fax: +525 (0)593 5194.

The Human Rights Centre, University of Essex, Wivenhoe Park, Colchester CO4 3SQ, UK. Fax: +44 (0)1206 974 598.

Human Rights Internet, 8 York Street, Suite 302, Ottawa, Ontario K1N 5S6, Canada. Fax: +6 (613) 789 7414. Website: http://www.hri.ca/

Human Rights Watch, 485 Fifth Avenue, New York NY 10017-6014, USA. Fax: +1 (212) 972 8400. Website: http://www.hrw.org/

International Centre for the Legal Protection of Human Rights, 33 Islington High Street, London N1 9LH, UK. Fax: +44 (0)171 278 4334.

International Committee of the Red Cross, 19 avenue de la Paix, 1202 Geneva, Switzerland. Fax: +41 (0)22 733 2057. Website: http://www.icrc.ch/

International Council on Social Welfare, 380 Saint Antoine Street West, Suite 3200, Montreal, Quebec H2Y 3X7, Canada. Website: http://www.icsw.org/

International Labour Organisation, 4 route des Morillons, 1211 Geneva 22, Switzerland. Fax: +41 (0)22 798 8685. Website: http://www.ilo.org/

Johns Hopkins University Press, Journals Publishing Division, 2715 North Charles Street, Baltimore MD 21218-4363, USA. Fax: +1 (410) 516 6968.

Kluwer Academic Publishers,
PO Box 17, 3300 AA Dordrecht,
The Netherlands.

Lokayan, 13 Alipur Road, New Delhi
110054, India.

Macmillan Press, Houndmills,
Basingstoke RG21 6XS, UK.
Fax: +44 (0)1256 842084.

Martinus Nijhoff Publishers,
PO Box 85889, 2508 CN The Hague,
The Netherlands.

Meulenhoff BV, Postbus 100, 1000 AC
Amsterdam, The Netherlands.

Minority Rights Group, 379 Brixton
Road, London SW9 7DE, UK. Website:
http://www.minorityrights.org/

The North–South Institute, 55 Murray
Street, Suite 200, Ottawa, Ontario K1N
5M3, Canada. Fax: +1 (613) 237 7435.

OMCT/SOS-Torture, 37-39 rue de
Vermont, 1211 Geneva 20, Switzerland.
Website: http://www.omct.org/

The Other India Press, Above Mapusa
Clinic, Mapusa 403507, Goa, India.

Oxfam Publications, Oxfam GB, 274
Banbury Road, Oxford OX2 7DZ, UK.
Fax: +44 (0)1865 313925.
Website: http://www.oxfam.org/

Oxford University Press (OUP),
Walton Street, Oxford OX2 6DP, UK.
Fax: +44 (0)1865 56646.

Pinter, Wellington House, 125 Strand,
London WC2R 0BB, UK.

Polity Press, 65 Bridge Street,
Cambridge CB2 1UR, UK.

Princeton University Press, 41 William
Street, Princeton, New Jersey NJ 08540,
USA. Fax: +1 (609) 258 6305.

**Raoul Wallenberg Institute for Human
Rights and Humanitarian Law,**
St Annegaten 4, 22350 Lund, Sweden.

Lynne Rienner Publishers, 1800 30th
St, Boulder, Colorado 80301, USA.
Fax: +1 (303) 444 0824.

Scarecrow Press Inc., 4720 Boston
Way, Lanham, Maryland 20706, USA.
Fax: +1 (301) 459 2118.

The South Centre, Chemin du
Champ-d'Anier 17, Case Postale 228,
1211 Geneva 19, Switzerland.
Fax: +41 (0)22 798 3433.

State University of New York Press,
State University Plaza, Albany NY
12246, USA.

Taylor and Francis Ltd, 1101 Vermont
Avenue NW, Suite 200, Washington DC
20005, USA.

Third World Network, International
Secretariat, 228 Macallister Road,
10400 Penang, Malaysia.
Fax: +60 (0)4 226 4505.

**Office of the UN High Commissioner
for Human Rights (UNHCHR),** Palais
des Nations, 8-14 avenue de la Paix,
1211 Geneva 10, Switzerland.
Website: http://www.unhchr.ch/

UN Development Programme (UNDP),
One United Nations Plaza, New York,
NY 10017, USA. Fax: +1 (212) 826 2058.
Website: http://www.undp.org/

UNESCO, 7 Place de Fontenoy, 75372
Paris 07 SP, France. Fax: +33 (0)1 456
71690. Website: http://www.unesco.org/

**United Nations High Commissioner
for Refugees (UNHCR),** Centre William
Rapard, 154 rue de Lausanne, 1202
Geneva, Switzerland.

Fax: +41 (0)22 739 8111.
Website: http://www.unhcr.ch/

United Nations Children's Fund (UNICEF), UNICEF House, 3 United Nations Plaza, New York, NY 10017, USA. Fax: +1 (212) 888 7465.
Website: http://www.unicef.org/

University of Florida Press, 15 Northwest 15th Street, Gainsville FL 32611, USA.

University of Pennsylvania Press, 418 Service Drive, Philadelphia PA 19104-6097, USA.

Vintage Books, 20 Vauxhall Bridge Road, London SW1X 2SA, UK. Fax: +44 (0)171 263 6127.

Westview Press, 5500 Central Avenue, Boulder, Colorado 80301-2877, USA. Fax: +1 (303) 449 3356.

The World Bank, 1818 H Street NW, Washington DC 20433, USA. Fax: +1 (202) 477 6391.

Zed Books, 7 Cynthia Street, London N1 9JF, UK. Fax: +44 (0)171 833 3960.

Development in Practice

Editor: *Deborah Eade, Oxfam GB*

Development in Practice is a forum
for practitioners, academics, and policy-
makers to exchange information and
analysis concerning the social dimensions
of development and humantarian work.
As a multi-disciplinary journal of policy
and practice, *Development in Practice*
reflects a wide range of institutional and
cultural backgrounds and a variety of
professional experience. All articles are
independently refereed.

Each issue brings together original
contributions from a wide range of
international sources, on themes which
have included armed conflict and development, environment, culture and development, participation and community
development, gender analysis, and
relations between NGOs, the State,
and multilateral agencies.

Development in Practice is published
quarterly by Carfax Publishing Limited
on behalf of Oxfam GB. Concessionary
rates are available for organisations from
developing countries.

Development
in Practice

Development in Practice Readers

Series Editor: *Deborah Eade*

Development in Practice Readers offer a selection of articles to promote debate on themes of current concern. Each paper has been chosen from *Development in Practice* — an international journal concerned with the social dimensions of development and humanitarian work, with contributions from practitioners, policy-makers, and researchers.

Each book in the series is introduced by a specially commissioned overview essay, and contains an annotated bibliography of current and classic titles which together constitute an essential reading list on the chosen theme.

Oxfam GB is registered as a charity no. 202918 and is part of Oxfam International

Titles already published

Development and Social Diversity (introduced by Mary B. Anderson, The Collaborative for Development Action)

Development in States of War (introduced by Stephen Commins, UCLA/World Vision International)

Development for Health (introduced by Eleanor Hill, community health consultant)

Development and Patronage (introduced by Melakou Tegegn, Panos East Africa)

Development and Rights (introduced by Firoze Manji, formerly Director of Amnesty International's Africa Programme)

Forthcoming in 1999

Development and Social Action (March 1999, introduced by Miloon Kothari, Habitat International Coalition)

Development with Women (September 1999, introduced by Dorienne Rowan-Campbell, DAWN)

Oxfam GB publishes a wide range of books, manuals, and resource materials for specialist, academic, and general readers.

For a free catalogue, please write to:
Oxfam Publishing
274 Banbury Road
Oxford OX2 7DZ, UK
telephone 01865 311311
e-mail publish@oxfam.org.uk

We welcome readers' comments on any aspects of Oxfam publications.

Please write to the editorial team at:
Oxfam Publications
274 Banbury Road
Oxford OX2 7DZ, UK